# Five Minutes, MR. BYNER!

## JOHN BYNER

### WITH DOUGLAS WELLMAN

Virginia

Published in the United States by WriteLife Publishing
(an imprint of Boutique of Quality Books Publishing Company, Inc.)
www.writelife.com

978-1-60808-234-6 (p)
978-1-60808-235-3 (e)

Library of Congress Control Number: 2020937558

Book Design by Robin Krauss, www.bookformatters.com
Cover Design by Rebecca Lown, www.rebeccalowndesign.com
Douglass Wellman author photo by Alisha Shaw

First editor: Michelle Booth
Second editor: Olivia Swenson

# DEDICATION

I've been fortunate to have a long career in a business I love. I've met wonderful people and developed enduring friendships, but when it comes to dedicating this book there is a special group I want to acknowledge: my family. I thank my talented wife, Annie Gaybis, for being at my side as a constant source of encouragement (and a lot of laughs). My children, Sandra, Donald, Rosine, and Patricia, are spread across the country, but always in my heart. I'm a lucky man.

# ACKNOWLEDGMENTS

The Beatles once said, "I get by with a little help from my friends." Well, that goes double for me. I want to thank the following people who helped with the preparation of this book by providing pictures, dates, and a little help when my memory stalled out.

Joanna Carson – for pictures and memories of my appearances on *The Tonight Show Starring Johnny Carson*.

Andrew Solt – who holds *The Ed Sullivan Show* recordings, for the use of pictures and research assistance.

Vincent Calandra – talent coordinator on *The Ed Sullivan Show,* for helping me get in touch with some of the people from the show and reminding me of our good times back then.

Steven Alexander – friend and computer expert, both of which I appreciate.

I'm grateful for your assistance.

John and Nathan Lane from "The Frogs."

# FOREWORD

## by Nathan Lane

T he immortal Sid Caesar once said, "Comedy has to be based on truth. You take the truth, and you put a little curlicue at the end."

And I suppose if you have enough curlicues, you've got an act.

There are so many comics these days, of all shapes and sizes and ethnic groups and sexualities and genders, in so many venues, from clubs to YouTube videos to podcasts to that perilous domain known as Twitter. So much so that it can be difficult to keep up with all the talented new original voices. It's hard to remember back to when there were only three major networks, and one boffo appearance on *The Tonight Show with Johnny Carson* could possibly change your life.

Let me come back to that.

It's 2004 and the phenomenal director/choreographer Susan Stroman and I were taking on an ambitious project at Lincoln Center Theater. I had always been fascinated by the musical version of *The Frogs*, which in its original form was the big hit play of 405 BC by Aristophanes. The musical was written by the wonderful Burt Shevelove and the incomparable Stephen Sondheim. They had very successfully and famously collaborated on *A Funny Thing Happened on the Way to the Forum*. *The Frogs*, however, was a very different animal—or slippery amphibian, shall we say—and because of its mixture of highbrow and lowbrow comedy, satire and political commentary, it made it an extremely tough nut to crack. In fact, when it was originally done in 1974, in the Yale swimming pool no less, it was not well received.

I wish someone had mentioned that to me.

Steve also said that because of the difficult acoustics, "It was like trying to perform a musical in a men's urinal." And I was not only starring in it, but doing a new adaptation of the book as well. What on earth was I thinking? I guess I was thinking I love a good challenge. Not to mention we were in a very politically divisive time in our country. Sound familiar?

Anyway, I had created a dual role for an actor—Charon, the pot-smoking, unflappable boatman on the River Styx, and Aeakos, the ancient and hearing-impaired guard at the gates of Hades. My initial inspiration for the part was Tim Conway and his "the Oldest Man" character on *The Carol Burnett Show*, which had always killed me. We inquired, but Mr. Conway was on a comedy tour with his best audience and co-star Harvey Korman. I kept thinking the part needed not just a good actor, but a great performer with a history in comedy and improvisation.

And then someone suggested John Byner. Or maybe I suggested him, I can't remember now. But the minute I heard his name, my eyes lit up. When I was a kid, my two older brothers, Dan and Bob, and I would always stay up late and tune in to *The Tonight Show* if John Byner was the guest. We *loved* John Byner like he was a sports hero, although I don't really follow sports, but there was no doubt he was a heavy hitter. He always seemed so relaxed and hip and full of fun and mischief. And he could make Johnny laugh. That was a big deal. I mean, really laugh, like prolonged laughter, where he threw his head back and twirled a little in his desk chair in delight.

The only other guests at that time who could make Carson laugh that hard were the legendary Don Rickles and Jonathan Winters. So, John Byner was in very rare company indeed, and it seemed like every appearance he had on *The Tonight Show* was boffo, at least at our house.

Also, John was, and still is, a sensational impressionist. And whether he was reminiscing about a local parish priest serving mass in Latin, who looked and sounded uncannily like John Wayne—"Aw, *Dominus vobiscum!*"—or demonstrating the hilarious break in Johnny Mathis's romantic singing voice, or becoming Ed Sullivan on his classic Sunday-night variety show running short on time and rushing everyone through their acts, like the Barzoni Brothers, Italian acrobats cut down to just one Barzoni apologizing in a thick accent—"It's not the same without my brother!"—or topping that, Ed Sullivan getting angry on his last show and saying everything he ever wanted to say, especially to the little Italian mouse, Topo Gigio, or memorably voicing the animated show *The Ant and The Aardvark*, where the ant sounded disturbingly like Dean Martin and the aardvark turned out to be a very excitable Jackie Mason, John's brilliance always shone through and knocked us out.

Perhaps his best and most popular impression back then was of veteran twentieth-century entertainer George Jessel. Often referred to as the Toastmaster General for his work as a master of ceremonies—"The Al Jolson funeral was widely attended by people just wanting to make sure"—he started in vaudeville and worked as a comedian and singer for many years. It's difficult to explain someone like George Jessel today. It's like going to the Museum of Natural History and pointing out the differences between the Cro-Magnons and the Neanderthals, but let's just say he was in the Al Jolson and Eddie Cantor category, if that rings a bell, telling ethnic jokes and singing schmaltzy songs like "My Mother's Eyes." I realize I've been dropping a lot of forgotten show business names, but please remember Google is your friend.

To say George Jessel was eccentric is an understatement. He often wore a military uniform on talk shows, maybe because he was the unofficial Toastmaster General, maybe because he used to entertain the troops during the Vietnam War, maybe because his good suit was in the dry cleaners, who the hell knows, and he had enough vocal and facial tics to initiate a set of clinical trials. Not to mention an incontrovertible toupee that looked like a tree monkey had fallen on his head and died of shock. Vocally he sounded a little like the love child of Buddy Hackett and Adam Sandler. Yikes, that's a troubling image I won't be able to get out of my head.

And yeah, I know, who's Buddy Hackett? I don't have time for all these questions, I'm writing a foreword for *John Byner*!

Anyway, John did this riotous and impeccable impression of Jessel, especially elderly Jessel, who, the older he got, became harder and harder to understand. Whatever noise was coming out of his mouth resembled someone trying to gargle in Yiddish while finishing an onion bagel. Okay, you had to be there. But John did this to perfection, and Carson would split a gut giggling, while the Lane brothers roared in Jersey City.

So I got Lincoln Center to offer him the part in *The Frogs* and got to work with one of my comedy heroes.

John went on to give an outstanding performance in the show and got singled out in all the reviews for his masterful deadpan comedy. He was a total pro and couldn't have been sweeter or more gracious, even when things weren't going so well.

During the run, before a matinee one afternoon, I said to

John, "Just for fun today, why don't you play Aeakos, the very old guard, as George Jessel? See if it works and we'll have a few laughs." John looked at me nervously and said, "Really?" And I said, "Yeah, what have we got to lose?" So John said, "Don't you want to rehearse?" And I said, "No, surprise me."

Cut to me knocking on these huge doors, they slowly open, and this little old man with long gray hair and an even longer beard steps out and starts talking like George Jessel. And it's uproariously funny. Unfortunately, even the prehistoric Lincoln Center subscribers, people who probably went to high school with Aristophanes, don't seem to remember George Jessel at all and remain silent. Perhaps even slightly puzzled that this guard from Hades sounds so, well, Jewish. Only one person is laughing and that's the great Paul Gemignani, our conductor and musical director, and he's beside himself. He was also a big John Byner fan and recognized immediately who he was doing. Then I started laughing, not just because of John's terrific impression, not just because Paul was in hysterics, but because I realized for the next few scenes John would have to continue being George Jessel. That absurdity really got me. Dear departed Georgie would have been so proud to know he was being resurrected on the Great White Way.

Later one of the young members of the ensemble asked me why the old guy was talking so funny at the matinee. I told him he may have had a stroke. Kids!

Obviously, John has had a remarkable career spanning decades, from doing comedy in small clubs in Greenwich Village to *The Ed Sullivan Show*—John will explain, Ed loved him—to *The Tonight Show with Johnny Carson,* to Steve Allen, who basically invented the talk show, to *The Carol Burnett Show*, to just about every major variety show or situation comedy there was on the air, to hosting his own variety show and introducing Bob Einstein as Super Dave Osborne, and on and on. But I'll let him tell you about all that.

And he's still going strong, as funny and as kind as ever. That's the truth without a curlicue.

Nathan Lane
Los Angeles, July 20, 2019

# Chapter One

## *I (Do) Know Jack*

Some people call it fate; others call it luck. Whatever you call it, you've probably been somewhere by chance at exactly the right moment and ended up getting a welcome surprise. I had one of those moments early in my career and it changed my life.

My ability to mimic voices opened up some special opportunities for me. Initially It was just a hobby. I entertained family members, school mates, buddies in the navy, and my coworkers in a myriad of blue-collar jobs, and one white-collar one. I had no idea my future would be in the spotlight in night clubs, television, cartoons, movies, variety shows, and a host of other exciting places. And maybe it wouldn't have been except for fate, luck, or whatever you want to call it. My world opened up one night because I happened to be on a little stage in New York at just the right moment. It was an unplanned event. Had it not occurred, I don't know where I'd be today.

When people think of the New York entertainment scene they usually think of Broadway. Broadway is more than just a street, it's a name that has become synonymous with the entire Theater District, and theater in general. While Broadway is the home for performers who are at the top of their game, there's a little area on the West Side of Lower Manhattan called Greenwich Village that has been the launching point for many a talented individual on their way up. It's several square blocks that most non-New Yorkers couldn't find on a map, but the name conjures up an aura of art, music, and counterculture to people all over the world. Greenwich Village "The Village" is a big deal.

In the '60s The Village was the place for me. Just below 11th Street on 7th Avenue South stands the Village Vanguard nightclub. Actually, it doesn't really stand, it kind of sinks. It's in a basement at the bottom of a dark, narrow staircase. My friend O. C. Smith once said, "You don't walk into that club, you fall into it." The space had been a Prohibition era speakeasy, but the end of Prohibition was bad news for the speakeasy business. This presented an opportunity for a man named Max Gordon. He leased the abandoned speak, got a legal liquor license, and went into the nightclub business in 1935. Keeping with the offbeat neighborhood culture, you could see almost anything on the Vanguard stage. Early on there were all styles of music and practically every other performing art, including poetry readings. Then came the bebop musicians and hipster artists of the '40s and '50s. Folk singers like Pete Seeger, Peter, Paul and Mary, and Burl Ives played the room. A young calypso performer by the name of Harry Belafonte got an early break there, as did jazz queen Eartha Kitt. I don't know if a professional yodeler ever played the room, but it wouldn't surprise me. Max liked comics, too, and Lenny Bruce, "Professor" Irwin Corey, and Wally Cox all played the Vanguard on their way to fame. The Vanguard is a big deal. It's especially a big deal to me, because in February of 1964 I was performing on the famous Vanguard stage.

The Vanguard isn't a big room. When you walk down the stairs you see a long, padded bench along the wall to your left, with a line of small cocktail tables. A few more tables are scattered in the middle of the room, with an open space for dancing. The bar is on the right. Dead ahead is a stage that seems ridiculously small for the size of talent that stands on it. They say good things come in small packages. That's the Vanguard.

In the early '60s the Vanguard was beginning a transition toward being primarily a jazz club. Like some of the other New York music rooms, the Vanguard would book comics to take the stage while the musicians were on a break. This worked out pretty well for me, since my manager, Harry Colomby, managed a couple of big jazz acts and had all the connections to the clubs. Max Gordon usually took a look at the performers before they got a shot at his stage, but in my case he took Harry's word for it that I was good enough for the room. I was always well received by the customers at the Vanguard so Max was happy. I was certainly happy and Harry was at least 10 percent as happy as I was.

You could see just about anything on the streets of the Village back then, which meant just about anyone could wander through the front door. After my set one night, Harry and I hung around for a quick drink. Afterwards I said goodbye and went to pick up my raincoat on the coatrack near the front door. It was gone. We spent a couple of minutes looking for it, but it was pretty clear that it had been stolen. As I was getting ready for a chilly walk to my car, there was a phone call to the office and a guy said, "If you're missing a raincoat, it's rolled up and in the doorway of the closed gas station across the street. It didn't fit." My lucky day—a considerate thief who wasn't my size.

I worked the Vanguard for the better part of a year, which was my longest ever club date. The audiences ranged from beatniks to businessmen, so I got to meet a lot of different people. One night I met a guy named Jack Babb. It was a brief conversation with lasting impact. Jack was the talent coordinator for *The Ed Sullivan Show*, and on 1960s TV Ed Sullivan was the biggest deal of them all.

In some ways *The Ed Sullivan Show* was like the early Vanguard. It was a variety show with no specific style of entertainment. If Ed thought someone was entertaining, no matter what they did, they had a shot at getting booked on the show. On any given Sunday night you could tune in and see a Broadway star and an opera singer, followed by a guy who spun plates on a stick. This strange format was genius back in the days when there were only three TV networks. If the viewer didn't like the act that was on they didn't turn the channel. They didn't have to; something different would be on soon. This TV free-for-all appealed to a huge audience and could make, and in a couple of cases break, careers.

Jack Babb was a distinctive man and a class act. He was about sixty years old and dressed like the cover of *GQ*. He had one of those low, rumbling voices that made everything sound important, whether he was reciting script notes or a restaurant menu. He wanted Sullivan to see me, and the best way to do that was for me to go to the theater on show day and perform in the dress rehearsal. This audition would be as close to the real thing as you could get. Jack laid out the prospects fairly simply. "If the old man likes you, we'll give you something in the future." Fair enough. It was Thursday and the dress rehearsal would be the next Sunday afternoon. That gave me almost three days to organize my best material, rehearse, and not let my nerves get in the way.

Sunday finally rolled around, so I put on my one and only suit, and drove from my home in Baldwin, Long Island, to pick up Harry in Forest Hills. It was a big day for both of us, since having one of his acts on the Sullivan show would boost his image as a manager. A rising tide lifts all boats, as they say. As we drove into Manhattan we talked about which bits I should use in my set and generally had a few laughs and a pretty good time. The car radio was playing softly in the background and Harry suddenly shouted, "They're ruining good music!" I said something like, "Huh?" and Harry twisted the volume control up until I heard the very distinctive voice of Joe Cocker singing "Cry Me A River." The song had been a huge hit when sung by the sultry Julie London, and jazz purist Harry was having nothing of Joe's guttural growl. He acted like he'd been poked with a cattle prod and I had to laugh at his reaction. Joe Cocker later became a good friend of mine. I don't know if Harry ever became a fan.

It took about twenty-five minutes to make the drive to the corner of 53rd and Broadway, a place that was then called Studio 50, but is now named the Ed Sullivan Theater in Ed's honor. It was around one o'clock when we parked around the corner and went into the theater looking for Jack. With 720 seats, the place was a pretty good size for comedy. Stand-up is intimate, so it's nice to have the audience close enough to see the expression on your face. The television cameras, microphone booms, and small army of staff and technicians milling around the scene were pretty impressive, but all the commotion was a bit unnerving. To ratchet up the tension level even more, the show wasn't recorded for later playback, it was broadcast live to TV stations around the country where millions of people watched as it happened.

Jack spotted us, greeted us, and gave us a brief outline of what was going to happen. Since I used music in my act, the first thing I needed to do was have a conference with Ray Block, who did the musical arrangements for the show and conducted the orchestra. Once we got the musical keys worked out, Jack took us upstairs to my dressing room where we got away from the pre-rehearsal commotion and I had a chance to focus on what I was going to do. We didn't sit too long. By two or three o'clock it was rehearsal time and I was on.

I went downstairs, got a few basic instructions from the stage manager, and waited for my cue. Honestly, after all these years I can't remember exactly what impressions I did. I had my music, so I did Frank Sinatra and Dean Martin. I probably did John Wayne—always a big hit in the clubs—and I certainly did my Ed Sullivan. Other than that I don't really recall. I guess I remember the overall experience of the lights, cameras, and big TV studio setting as a whole more than individual bits. I finished my set to applause and headed back upstairs to my dressing room feeling relieved and pretty good about the whole thing. In a few minutes there was a knock at the door and Jack walked in with a smile.

"Hey," he said. "The old man likes you. You go on tonight."

Tonight?!

Fate, luck . . . whatever you want to call it, I've had my share. There's a lot of great talent working the hotel lounges of the country only because they didn't get the break required to move up the line. Jack Babb's decision to stop by the Vanguard that night was the bit of luck I needed to give my career a boost. If that hadn't happened, maybe I would have gotten another break, or maybe I wouldn't have. Who knows?

Here's a big surprise for you: life can be difficult. Oh . . . I guess you knew that. Everyone has their ups and downs and I've had mine, too, but you're not going to read about them here. You have your own problems; you don't need to hear me complaining about mine. Besides, that's what the *National Enquirer* is for. No, I'd rather talk about the good things in life, the fun things, the uplifting things. I've had an exciting life among fascinating and talented people, and I'm still out there having a ball. I've had a lot of laughs. That's what I want to share with you. In the world of entertainment, some of the funniest and most fascinating things happen in places the audience never sees. I'm going to take you there.

This will also be a bit of an entertainment history book. Although I was still pretty young, I got to work with some of the pioneers in television, like Ed Sullivan and Steve Allen. Variety shows were popular for a long time and I shared stages with Bob Hope, Bing Crosby, Glen Campbell, Andy Williams, Sammy Davis, Diana Ross, and on and on. I even had a variety show of my own. I was a cast member on the offbeat sitcom *Soap*, and made thirty-seven appearances on *The Tonight Show* starring Johnny Carson, when Johnny was the undisputed king of late-night television. There was no such thing as a bad *Tonight Show*. Las Vegas was still in its relative infancy, but its showrooms drew the best of the best. When you drove down the Strip you saw real entertainers, celebrities who were so big they only needed one name: Frank, Dean, and of course, Elvis. I was there and I got to be a part of all of it, and for that I'm grateful.

So, I'm going to share some stuff from my life and the great people I've been blessed to have in it. But just the good stuff. In the end, that's the only stuff that really counts.

# Chapter Two
## *Kid Stuff*

I came from a normal family. I hope that doesn't disappoint you. A lot of celebrities go on talk shows to discuss their books and whine about their abusive father, alcoholic mother, or uncle who lived in the attic and practiced the bugle. I don't have any of that. If there was any disadvantage in my life, it was being the fifth of six children who were all competing for the affection of our parents. I really can't complain about that either, since that was part of the motivation for developing my voice talents.

My father's name was Michael Biener, but the family name was originally Buehner. Somewhat prophetically, the name means "stage." In the nineteenth and beginning of the twentieth centuries, the United States was the place to go. It seemed like the whole world had tilted and everyone who wasn't attached to a good life in their own country slid toward America. They landed in a pile on Ellis Island in New York Harbor where all immigrants from Europe were processed. So it was with my grandfather, John Buehner. He earned his passage to the United States by working as a ship's cook. He was born in Biene, Germany, in 1887, so he apparently either decided to honor his hometown by changing his name from Buehner to Biener, or someone in immigration decided to do it for him. With his new country and new name he set out on a successful career as a carpenter. He was also pretty successful as a family man, fathering six children. He died in 1937, the year I was born, so I never got to know him.

My father was a great guy and something of a mechanical genius. I think he probably could have taken a handful of paperclips and turned them into an engine. That was his real talent; he was a wizard with engines. When I was young we lived in the Laurelton neighborhood of the borough of Queens, where he made his living as a truck mechanic for Queens County. He left that job when we moved to Merrick, Long Island, for about a year, the first of several moves. Dad's golden touch with engines drew the attention of the car racing community, who used his talents to tune their cars. They'd haul them out to him on flatbed trucks, and he'd tweak the engines until they reached maximum power. He was lucky to have a career and a side business doing what he truly enjoyed.

My parents kept a secret from us kids to save us from worry. Dad was ill, but we didn't realize it until he became unable to work. Even then I don't think we realized the seriousness of the situation. My three oldest siblings had started lives of their own and were no longer living at the house, so our parents decided to move us out farther on the Island to Bohemia. There they purchased five acres of land with two houses on it for $5,000. Try making that deal today. We lived in the front house and rented out the other, but finally sold the front house and moved into the back one. This turned out not to be such a great idea. The back house was really just an uninsulated summer house and not adequate for the cold Long Island winter. We ended up huddling around an old oil stove in the living room, which was inconvenient, but oddly enough, it's one of my favorite childhood memories. Dad was a great guitar player and he had taught Mom to play the mandolin. That winter became a family song fest with all of us gathered around the stove, singing and generally having a ball. That happy time really brought us together as a family. When Dad died shortly thereafter at the age of forty-six we were all devastated.

Dad's death triggered another move. Mom still had three kids at home to feed and raise, so she couldn't just sit around and mourn. She solved the immediate problem by accepting an invitation from our Aunt Annie and her husband Joe to stay with them in Elmhurst, Queens. There my brother Tom and I went to PS 89, and our sister Christine went to Newtown High School. Mom's first job in Queens was working nights at Bellevue Hospital. Soon she was able to put some money together and we were able to move into a one-bedroom apartment in a new building. It was only six blocks from PS 89 on McNish Street and a block from the 8th Avenue subway line. Mom and Christine took the bedroom and Tom and I shared a couch that pulled out into a bed. That was just fine with us.

Mom was a strong, dedicated, loving mother. She was born Christina Marie Ball, and she meant the world to us. Her lineage was Irish and she had a great sense of humor. She married Dad when she was only seventeen and raised six kids. As we moved across Long Island, her jobs changed with our location. A few years after WWII, she worked in a factory where they made an assortment of safety flares for ships, trains, and traffic. Some of them created smoke for daytime use and some a bright red light for night. There was a slight problem, however. The chemicals caused her skin to turn orange. Not the ideal career. She was an attendant at the Islip State Hospital when my father died, and then took a job at Bellevue Hospital in Queens. She didn't like working nights, so she found employment answering the phone for the

NY Mets at Shea Stadium. Someone from the Yankees called one day and liked the way she answered the phone, so he offered her a job for more money. We always said that the Mets had traded her to the Yankees. She developed a "telephone operator voice" that seemed to be so typical of women in that occupation in those days. It was the voice Lily Tomlin used for her Ernestine the telephone operator character on *Rowan and Martin's Laugh-In* ("Good gracious, hello. Is this the party to whom I am speaking?"). Mom would occasionally break into that cadence in conversations at the house, which was always good for a laugh. She was working for the Yankees when she died at the age of sixty-nine. The Yankee organization sent a huge floral display to her funeral. She meant a lot to them, too.

Families back then, particularly Catholic families, tended to have a lot of children. We were no exception. Miriam was the first born. She was sharp and motivated and became a secretary for a buyer at JCPenney when she was only nineteen. Min, as we called her, was always creative. Once they had a promotion for Arrow shirts and she came up with the slogan "Buy your beau an Arrow." Pretty clever. At twenty-two she got married and she and her husband, Stan, had six boys. I'm happy to say that she's still active at the age of ninety-four. She and my sister Christine travel all over the country and love to hit Manhattan for a Broadway show. Miriam can still dance a pretty mean Lindy, too.

Helen was the next born, a very devout Catholic from an early age. So much so that she decided to become a nun and entered a religious order at the age of fourteen. She seemed pretty happy with this decision for a while, and ultimately served for fourteen years, but lifelong commitments are not always best made while still a teenager. She eventually felt it wasn't the right thing for her, and Pope Pious XII gave her permission to leave the order. She went on to become a wife and mother.

Next was my oldest brother, Michael. After my father's death he became a surrogate father to my younger brother Tom and me while remaining a fun-loving big brother with a dash of craziness thrown in. He lived in Bohemia and would drive in to surprise us. He had a tremendous sense of humor, and I treasure the memories of the times I spent with him laughing. He was always up for something spontaneous, like a last-minute camping trip upstate to a town called Phoenicia, where we hiked and laughed and threw lines in the water for the pretty much non-existent fish. Michael had been a paratrooper and was injured in a jump. His recovery was slow and required frequent trips to the Veterans Administration Hospital for treatment. This didn't slow him down one bit; in fact, it seemed to enhance the zaniness already in his character. He lived for clothes and cars and some of my fondest memories are the times when we went roaring off in his convertible with the top down, regardless of the weather. Somewhere along the line we had acquired a collection of colorful costume hats, so Michael, Tom, and I would go racing across Long Island laughing, our goofy hats blowing in the wind. It didn't occur to me until many years later that some of our more unusual experiences may have been fueled by the pain medication being doled out to Michael at the VA. Whatever. We had a wonderful time and I wouldn't trade those memories for anything.

Michael also had a gift for doing vocal effects. One of them in particular turned into a long-running gag. He could speak in a bizarre, high-pitched voice. When he spoke with a straight face in a casual manner, it was really weird but still believable.

The best part was I could do the same voice. Aside from being fun to do, the squeaky voice made a great vengeance tool for waiters and waitresses who disliked having to wait on kids unaccompanied by parents. They were easy to spot, since they usually started with the bad attitude the moment they stepped up to the table. "Whadda you two want?" they'd fire off at us like a sentry challenge. That was Michael's cue to go into action.

"Let's see," he would begin in a slow, deliberate voice that sounded like it was squeezing out from a too-tight collar. "I'd like a hamburger, french-fried po-ta-toes, and a coke-a-cola." This always stopped the server in their tracks. Then they would slowly turn to me, a little stunned, and ask for my order.

"I'll have the saaaaame thing," I would squeak in the same voice. Game over. Kids two, waiter zero.

Christine was next. Just as Michael had become a surrogate father, Christine became a second mother to us. While we were living in the one-bedroom apartment in Elmhurst, Queens, Mother had to leave early in the morning to go to work. This left two young boys who had to get ready for school, and they sure weren't going to do it on their own. At least not on time. Christine stepped in and got us put together, changed our bed back into a couch, and got us out the door and moving in the right direction. She eventually met a New York City police officer named Bill Cook, and they got married. I was in the navy on their wedding day, stationed in Bainbridge, Maryland, and without a car. Back then they had pickup stations across from the base where service men could catch a ride going east or west. Any patriotic traveler passing by could stop and give us a lift. A young sailor in uniform didn't have much trouble catching a ride. I got lucky right away when the first guy that came along happened to be another sailor and I got a ride all the way to Long Island. There was one slight glitch in the trip. We stopped for gas and I ran in for a bar of ice cream, which immediately began melting and dripped chocolate on my summer whites. I cleaned it up as best I could. *No one's perfect*, I told myself.

Thanks to the sailor, who drove like a madman, I got to the wedding on time and proudly showed up in my slightly smudged uniform. No one cared. I could have been covered in paint. They were just glad to see me. Christine and Bill made a fine couple and the ceremony was great. Then came the reception where I experienced the second slight glitch of the day. Despite the reputation some sailors have, I was very naïve. At the reception there was the traditional round of toasts from everyone—"To the bride, to the groom, to children," etc. By the time they got to me they'd toasted everything but the weather. Being a budding comedian, I decided to go for a joke. I raised my Manhattan cocktail glass, with the cherry in the bottom, and proclaimed, "To the cherry!" A silence fell over the room. Then, after a couple of seconds, a roar of laughter erupted. I was unaware that cherry was a euphemism for a certain part of the female body that would be particularly significant on a wedding night. When it was explained to me later I was mortified.

I was the next child in line, but you'll hear plenty about me later, so we'll move on to the youngest in the family, Tom. Tom and I, being the brothers closest in age, were constant companions. Our many moves were usually during the summer school break, so when we started our new school in the fall we were the only people we knew. I used to say that we were stuck with each other. If it's possible to be closer than brothers, we are. He was my best friend then and remains so now. We were kids at a time when every free moment wasn't spent staring at a smartphone. We had a bit of a Tom Sawyer childhood at a time when life and its pleasures were simpler.

One day we decided to ride our bikes over to Oakdale to try our luck at fishing. There was a private hunting and fishing club there, which we could only aspire to join in our dreams. However, whenever there was a big rain storm the private pond would overflow and spill speckled trout over a waterfall and off the club property. There was also an ideally placed railroad trestle that provided a perch for us to drop our lines from into the river below and snag the newly liberated trout. Tom and I were happily fishing away when I pulled up my hook and discovered that some smart fish had gotten my bait and left me with an empty hook. I sat down on the train track to reload another worm when a huge trout rose to the surface and Tom yelled at me to come look. I jumped up and ran to the side of the trestle just as a train came roaring around the curve and onto the bridge, blasting right through where I had been sitting. Because of the thick woods adjacent to the track and the roar of the waterfall, we couldn't see or hear the train coming. I reached the side of the trestle just in time to turn and see my fishing pole smashed into a hundred pieces as the train barreled by me with mere inches to spare. I stood there in shock. I could have been in a hundred pieces. Thank God for Tom and that trout. Tom went on to be a successful television writer, which was great since neither one of us would have made a living as a fisherman.

Another favorite adventure was sneaking out of the house in the middle of the night. I was about thirteen when we lived in Queens, and Tom and I would quietly slip out of the house at 3:00 a.m., being careful not to wake Christine. We'd meet up with our friend Jerry Cole, sneak under the subway turnstile, and make our way to the 59th Street Bridge where we'd trek into Manhattan. The objective was to see how many plays we could get from the pinball machines on Broadway with our meager pocket change. The total investment was usually around a quarter. Then it was back over the bridge and into the house around 6:00 a.m. before the sun rose and Mom came home from work.

Like most kids, I picked up a nickname. Biener was pronounced beaner, so my nickname became Beans. I had friends in all of the many neighborhoods we lived in, and childhood was pretty enjoyable. But life is life, and bad things happen. My school class was taking a trip to a local lake and I had to get permission from my mother to go swimming. She felt that the water was too cold and refused to sign a permission slip, leaving me more or less shore bound to watch. I had a friend named Kenny who was a few years older than I was and had a crush on my sister Christine. I was wading on shore looking for tadpoles while Kenny and some guys in his class were out several yards in a boat. Kenny decided to do a little diving demonstration, supposedly for me, but in reality to impress Christine.

"Hey, Beans," he yelled. "Watch this!" With that he executed a pretty good dive off the boat. I smiled and went back to my tadpole hunt. About ten seconds later there was a chorus of shouting. "He didn't come back up!" There was an immediate ruckus of people coming to his rescue and gathering around to see what was going on and I was caught up in it. They got him out of the water, but it didn't end well. Kenny died. We found out later that he had a heart problem that neither he nor his family were aware of. When he dove into the frigid water his heart stopped. You're never prepared for something like that, especially as a kid.

For the most part, my childhood rolled on in a fairly pleasant and normal manner. The first hint that I might be a bit different came early in my life. This was in the days before television, so the radio was our primary source of entertainment, but a trip to the local movie house was always a treat. In those days they had children's movies, ones that didn't feature things getting blown up, naked people, scary aliens, or naked people and scary aliens getting blown up. We had *National Velvet*, starring a young Elizabeth Taylor who stole my juvenile heart. Then there was *My Friend Flicka*, *Dumbo*, and the *Lassie* movies, which we kids could relate to in the much gentler world of my youth. The movies were a world of magic. I remember seeing a newsreel of a football game and some of the footage was in slow-motion. I asked my mother how they could be moving so slowly. Rather than explain the whole thing, she told me they had special shoes. Boy, did I want those shoes!

The first film I saw that wasn't specifically a children's movie was when my mother took us to see *Here Come the Waves* when I was six years old. It doesn't appear on any top ten film lists, but it is notable for one thing. The movie's star, Bing Crosby, sang a song called "Ac-Cent-Tchu-Ate the Positive," which earned an Academy Award nomination, and a later recording of it sold a ton of records. The thing that fascinated me was that Bing also danced as he sang. I'd seen people sing and dance before, but Bing had some particularly neat moves that really captured my sense of excitement. When we got home my father asked what the movie was about and Christina suggested that I explain it. At that point I launched into a Bing Crosby impression, singing the song and dancing the moves as best I remembered them. No one saw that coming. My living room performance drew surprise and appreciative applause from the family. From that point on, whenever we had company, I was asked to perform. Being singled out in our big family was a real ego boost. I had found something that I enjoyed doing and people enjoyed watching me do. I soon expanded my act by impersonating cartoon voices.

Having a talent, especially a talent that makes people laugh, is a great way to make friends for a kid who changes schools often. I had gone to six schools before I left high school. The first school I attended was a Catholic school, so impersonations of the sisters who ran the school were always particularly popular, at least with the students. The nuns were not all known for their sterling sense of humor. In those days a brisk crack across the knuckles with a wooden ruler was the means of reminding little boys who the boss was. Of course, sneaking these performances in behind their backs made the whole thing even funnier.

Moving is not usually a lot of fun, and moving a lot is a lot less fun. On our frequent treks across Long Island, we occasionally found ourselves in unusual circumstances. When we moved from Laurelton it wasn't to go directly to North Merrick. The North Merrick house was not vacated in time by the owners, so my parents brought us to the home of friends, the Dojat family in Corona, Long Island, to wait it out. Our family was slightly reduced at this point. Helen was already in the convent and Miriam, the eldest, decided to stay back in Laurelton with her girlfriend's family. That left Mom and Dad; Michael, age sixteen; Christine, age twelve; me, age seven; and Tom age five. It was pretty decent of the Dojats to take our brood in. It wasn't like they could just throw a pillow and blanket on the couch and be done with it. There were a lot of us.

The Dojats owned a combination store-home like we used to see in small rural communities. It was a store front with their house connected in the rear. You entered the home through a door in the back of the store. There was also a side door that went directly into the house from outside. Fortunately for us, at this time the store was not operating so it was a big empty room. We, along with the furniture from the Laurelton house, stayed in the empty store front. The store front had big glass display windows that had been soaped over so you couldn't see in, but during the night the illumination of the streetlight would cast a shadow on the glass of anyone walking by. In order to use a restroom, one would have to enter the house from the store and walk across their living room to reach it. It's sometimes hard enough to make your way through a strange place in the dark of night, but just to make the whole trip more interesting, the Dojats had a dog.

Very early one morning, before dawn, we awoke from our various places of rest to see a human figure outside pressed against the huge whitewashed window, and calling, "Mom, Dad help," with arms waving desperately, like a large bird trying to take off or an angel (if angels yell. I don't know, I never had the opportunity to check). We looked around to see that Christine was not in her bed. Mom, realizing the figure out there had to be her, rushed to let her in. Seeing Christine standing there in her night shirt on that cold, dark morning, Mom cried out what she always did in shocking situations: "Jesus, Mary, and Joseph!" I think it was her way of calling in reinforcements.

After Mom brought Christine inside and threw a blanket around her shoulders to warm her up, Christine explained that she had gone through the store's back door to use the facility. In trying to exit the bathroom, she was confronted by the Dojat's growling dog, who refused to let her back into the living room. In desperation, she crawled outside through the bathroom window and ran around to the street to try to get in touch with us through the store front. Not the greatest way to wake up. The Dojats were wonderful people. The dog . . . not so much.

Having an audience of any size, whether it was my family in our living room or my classmates in school, was a great motivator for honing my talent. As I mentioned before, a kid in a big family can get lost, so having a talent that draws attention is a real ego boost. And it was fun. We were living in Corona and I was in the second grade of Catholic school when I got my first opportunity to appear in an actual organized show. The class was performing a play called *Billy Boy* and I was picked to be the lead. This was my "Bing Moment." I got to perform a catchy little chorus. The rest of the cast sang:

*Can she bake a cherry pie, Billy Boy, Billy Boy?*
*Can she bake a cherry pie, charming Billy?*

And I, Billy, sang in response:

*She can bake a cherry pie like a cat can wink an eye.*
*She's a young thing and cannot leave her mother.*

Not only was I thrilled at the prospect of performing in front of a real audience, but I was having an absolute blast at the rehearsals. There was only one small fly in the ointment: we were going to move again before opening night. We only lived there three months. I was enjoying the whole experience so much that I didn't want to tell the nuns that I wouldn't be there for the actual show because, obviously, they would replace me. So the solution to the problem seemed simple. I just didn't tell them until we moved, which happened to be the day before the performance. As you can imagine, this seriously rocked the *Billy Boy* boat. Fortunately, another stage-struck student had been watching the rehearsals with a keen, perhaps envious, eye and was able to step right into my role. This made everyone feel better. Best of all, I had a load of fun before I headed off to North Merrick with my family.

My vocal talent was earning me a lot of positive attention and laughs. Laughter is almost like a drug. When you can make people laugh, when you can make them happy, when people come up to you and ask you to perform, the experience is addictive. The natural response to this is to do more things and do them all better. A concert pianist spends hours every day at the piano perfecting that talent. Fortunately, I didn't need a piano. They're hard to carry around. My two "practice instruments" were the radio and movies. Cartoon voices were always popular with my friends. I still do cartoon voices today, but in a different way. A good piece of my career has been spent creating those voices rather than mimicking them. I've created the voices for a world of characters from ants to aliens. It is an entirely different kind of thrill to look at a piece of animation and imagine how that character should sound and then create the voice. I've also been called upon to mimic a celebrity voice and apply it to a cartoon character. That is why the lazy Ant sounds like Dean Martin and the nervous Aardvark sounds like Jackie Mason in *The Ant and the Aardvark*. And in case you're wondering, both Dean and Jackie approved of the voices. I'm happy to call them my friends, and I think they kind of got a kick out of it. It's been huge fun. Not everyone gets paid to be an aardvark.

Talent contests were a big thing when I was a kid. There

were talent contests because we didn't have TV until I was a teenager. Now TV is all talent contests. Who woulda thought? Talent contests back then, both local and national, were frequently on the radio, which was a big deal. A mass audience always draws interest, so talent contests, whether they were on the radio or not, became very popular with the public. It seemed like every community had one. I'd been getting a great response performing in living rooms and classrooms, so I decided it was time to take my act on the road. Not very far on the road, but on the road nevertheless. Any community within commuting distance for a fourteen-year-old boy was an opportunity for me to perform. I generally did very well through the auditions and made my way to the finals. On contest nights, the other acts backstage, my competitors, assured me that I had to be the winner. But I didn't win. The winners always seemed to be the child of a local politician, banker, or big businessman. It didn't take me too long to see the pattern, and there was a good lesson in it. There is no rule that says life has to be fair. Armed with that knowledge one can do one of two things: quit or push on. I was having way too much fun to quit, so push on I did. That's when I learned another lesson. If you keep working you eventually turn the odds in your favor. In some way maybe those contests I didn't win as a teenager were just another step on the ladder for winning as an adult.

School provided another valuable life lesson for me. As I mentioned, from the time I started in first grade until the time I went off to the navy, I attended six different schools. That's like constantly being out on an audition. That's a lot of different teachers, a lot of different kids, and a lot of different impersonations of cartoon characters that helped me become one of the gang instead of "the new kid." All of this school changing seemed to leave me with a desire to belong to something more permanent. High school wasn't cutting it for me anymore and I was looking for something else, preferably with a little excitement. Since my brother Michael had served in the military and told me a few stories, I was aware that being in the service was a good way to learn something that might later actually turn into a civilian career. I liked the ocean and the opportunity to see the world was tempting, so I dropped out of high school and off to the naval recruiter's office I went.

On March 15, 1955, at three o'clock in the morning, I stepped off a bus from Whitehall Street into the Naval Training Center at Brainbridge, Maryland, and lined up with a group of somewhat tense and slightly sleepy young men. The next step was dismantling us as kids and rebuilding us as sailors through the process of boot camp. From that point on it was like being on a treadmill of discipline, physical training, and educational classes. When we rolled off the other side we would officially be seamen.

For the most part I liked boot camp. There's great camaraderie in being part of a military unit, and I enjoyed learning everything from tying knots to ship recognition. I even liked drilling. There were drilling contests where we competed against other barracks as we marched to class. The best marching barracks won an award. I liked working as a team to be the best. Not everything was perfect, of course. It was my first time away from my family and I certainly missed them, but it's just one of those things that goes with the territory. I had another thing going for me in boot camp. I played the harmonica and that, combined with my impersonations, earned me a little consideration from my barracks mates. They were happy to have the entertainment, so they responded by doing things for me like washing my clothes and taking care of some of the more mundane aspects of service life. The whole thing was fun and worked out for all involved.

After boot camp, I was sent off to radioteletype school. There I had another appreciative audience for my impressions. I did my usual repertoire of movie stars and cartoon characters. Taking a little poke at authority is always popular so, as I had with the nuns in school, from the time I entered boot camp I began impersonating officers. This has its risks. In grade school it's called being a bad boy and earned a rap on the knuckles. In the military it's called insubordination and could earn you a trip to the brig.

One afternoon an ensign walked into the barracks and told me that he'd heard I did an impersonation of him and he wanted to hear it. He was on his rounds inspecting barracks to make sure that all was in order, that no one was smoking where prohibited, and that there were no fires or other disasters that needed to be dealt with, and there apparently was a lull in the action. This was my first "command" performance. Fortunately, he had a sense of humor and wanted to hear it for entertainment value not disciplinary action. To get the most from my performance he handed me his hat and whistle. He was a good audience. He was really laughing it up when a siren suddenly sounded, notifying everyone that something had gone wrong. He immediately bolted for the door, leaving me wearing his hat and whistle. I had to chase him down outside to give him his gear back.

Another time I was mimicking the walk of one of the officers. He strutted like Popeye, with his chest thrust forward and his rear end thrust back. I was doing my impersonation of him for the guys when they abruptly stopped laughing. I turned around to see why, and there was the officer I was impersonating, standing behind me. This is the kind of thing that can turn out really badly. I froze and waited for his reaction. I guess the shocked expression on my face struck him as funny and he laughed instead of taking offense.

While in radioteletype school some of the guys in the barracks decided that I should audition for the base talent show. That seemed like a pretty good idea, so I headed off to see the officer in charge of the show with a few of my comrades trailing behind as a show of support. I entered the office and stood at attention as my fan club waited at the open door. The officer had his chair turned with his back to me, staring out a window, as he spoke with someone on the telephone. I waited patiently. And waited. And waited. I looked back at my friends in the doorway, not sure of what to do next. They gestured that I should do something to get his attention, so I put my hands on his desk, leaned forward, and whispered, "Sir . . ." That definitely got his attention. He spun around in his swivel chair and yelled, "Take your hands off my *desk*!" I snapped to attention with a quick "Yes, Sir!" gave a salute and a quick about face and got out of there fast. To add insult to injury, when we attended the base talent show a month later we saw that there wasn't anyone too special in the field. In the immortal words of Marlon Brando in *On the Waterfront*, "I could have been a contender."

Finally, all of the drilling and training was complete. I think we were all pretty proud. I know I was. Most of us had taken a big step from being insecure adolescents to confident young men. That was a pretty big accomplishment in only nine weeks of boot camp and six months of specialized training. I also had a new job classification: I was a radioman. Operating a radio is a long way from performing on it, but when you're eighteen you take what you can get.

At last it was time to go out with the fleet. The question was, where? It's a big world and the United States Navy is all over it. Our billets—locations where we would be stationed—were determined by our school grades. The billets were written on a blackboard and, one by one, in descending order of our grades, we picked where we wanted to go. We could choose Hawaii, Japan, the Philippine Islands, and a lot of other exciting places, but the choicest billets would be grabbed by the guys with the best test scores. The rest of the guys would get what was left, billets like the frosty Aleutian Islands and some places we had never heard of. This was when one of those good news-bad news things happened. The bad news: I wasn't exactly at the top of my class, so the odds of going to some tropical paradise were unlikely. The good news: I had a lot of friends. There was a guy in our group named Roy Cloutier. Roy was liked by all, but Roy and I had a special way of making each other and the rest of the guys laugh. Everyone knew Roy and I would like to be stationed together, but Roy was near the top of the class, so he was going to be picking a billet before I was. When Roy picked San Diego, the word went out to the guys: lay off San Diego. Save it for John. When my turn came up San Diego was still open and off I went to the West Coast. It was pretty decent of the guys to do that for me and I appreciated it.

My first assignment was to the submarine tender USS *Nereus*, AS17, assigned to Squadron Five. Many United States Navy vessels are named after prominent Americans, but in this case the name comes from an ancient Greek term for "the old man of the sea." The *Nereus* was 529 feet long with a crew of about 1,200. We were anchored in San Diego Bay, so submarines from the fleet that needed repair or resupply would pull alongside and tie up to us or one another. There were times when we serviced as many as twenty subs at a time, and you could walk from boat to boat right down the line. One of my jobs was to deliver mail to the subs, and I can tell you for an absolute fact that that's as close to being on one as I wanted to come. I love the ocean, but I prefer to be on top of it, not submerged in a metal cylinder for weeks or months at a time.

After three or four months, Roy Cloutier and I were both transferred to the USS *Florikan,* a submarine rescue vessel that was tied up at the foot of Broadway in San Diego before we set sail. This was a much smaller ship at about 250 feet long with a crew of only about 100, and it had a very specific mission. When they called it a "rescue vessel," they weren't kidding. The ship was fitted with a diving bell, a capsule that could be lowered onto the hatch of a sunken sub. Once secured to the deck, sailors trapped in the sub could enter the capsule through the hatch and be pulled to the surface. This is pretty heroic stuff and not a job for just anyone. We all took serving on this ship very seriously. Roy and I served together on the *Florikan* for a few months until he shipped out to Adak, Alaska, the next of his many assignments on what became a career in the navy.

I joined the USS *Florikan* as a radioman and looked forward to the adventure. Being on a ship at sea is a different world from being on base. When you get off duty you can't drive into town to see a movie or have a beer, and the accommodations on a smaller ship are anything but spacious. At any given moment on a ship there's a whole bunch of young guys with a little time on their hands. Young guys with time on their hands can be a problem anywhere, but particularly in the close confinement of a ship. The navy is well aware of this and provides diversions to occupy the seamen's free time and keep morale as high as possible. One of the activities was a show commonly known as a Smoker. It was like a talent contest without the contest. Sailors and marines who had a talent would perform for the other sailors and marines on the ship. Sometimes the crews of several ships gathered to watch the show.

When I first boarded the USS Florikan I was greeted by an ensign named Karabel, who was in charge of the radio shack. He was a great help in getting me squared away. After he got to know me, he thought I would make a great addition to the ship's Smoker, so he told me that he would inform the captain. He returned the next day with the captain's response. "I told the captain that you do impersonations," he reported as I waited expectantly, "and he asked if you could impersonate a radioman." Not everyone appreciates talent.

Since I'd enlisted before I was eighteen years old, I qualified for what we referred to as a Kiddie Cruise—we didn't serve a full four years. So, after an interesting and exciting forty-two months, my naval career sailed off into the sunset and I was once again a civilian. I found myself in the same place as when I left high school.

I needed a job.

# Chapter Three
## *Post-Naval Drift*

In May of 1958 I was once again a civilian walking the streets of Long Island. I was four years older, four years wiser, and I'd had a lot of practice performing my act for my sailor buddies. What I didn't have was money. If I was going to continue to enjoy the good things of life, like eating and living indoors, I was going to need to get a job.

I'd earned my GED in the navy and the obvious place to start looking for work was by trying to market my naval training as a radioteletype operator. That didn't turn out as well as I'd hoped. The only interested employer I could find was Western Union, and they paid a whopping thirty-five dollars a week. That's about what it cost for a week's round-trip fares on the Long Island Railroad from my home in Rockville Centre to Manhattan.

Performing was the one thing I really enjoyed, but it seemed like an impossible dream. It was one of those "you can't get there from here" situations. How does an average guy get his name in lights? Impossible. They don't put help-wanted ads for comedians in the *New York Times*. What I needed was something steady to pay the bills while my show business plan—or complete lack of one—simmered in the background. I'm sure most of you have been out of work at one time or another. It's not a great feeling. On the other hand, I was young and didn't have any real responsibilities other than caring for myself, so there wasn't an enormous amount of pressure on me. I had one other big advantage: I didn't really care what I did. Since I didn't have a particular career in mind, I didn't have to focus on a specific industry. All I had to do was start knocking on doors. Any door. Any job I could land was good enough for the time being. Job hunting is a little easier when you're not too fussy.

My persistent door knocking eventually led me to Transport Clearings, a company that was in the business of collecting overdue freight bills for truckers. They were looking to take on a trainee to work in the back office, and I showed up at the right moment. Today that job would be called technical support, but back then it was called "guy who knows how to fix the photocopy machine." It was actually a pretty decent job. The people were all nice and, surprisingly for the time, women outnumbered men about eight to one. I followed the standard path for business back then: I started in the mail room and worked my way up. I had the opportunity to try out new material on my colleagues once in a while, but mostly I just did my job and tried to do it as best I could. That's where the problem arose. I got promoted. I got a desk, a telephone, and a list of people who hadn't paid their bills. My job was to call them and dun them for money.

There are certain people who are extremely good at this kind of work, and others who are extremely bad. I fall into the second category. I think everyone should pay their bills, but let's face it, stuff happens and sometimes you get caught short. Emotionally, I'm a little on the soft side. This is why my act is always gentle and not mean. I'm not a mean guy. I just don't have it in me, even when I'm in the right and it's my job. Suddenly every day became a gut-twisting experience as I called people and listened to their personal horror stories and why they couldn't pay their bills. Eventually it got to me. I felt bad for these people, so I took the bills for the people with the worst stories and moved them to the bottom of the pile. Every time they reappeared at the top I moved them back to the bottom. It was pretty clear that I was not cut out for this line of work, and nothing good would come of it for me or my employer. It was time to move on.

There was another little motivator in my decision to change jobs. I got married. I met a young woman named Eleanor Belcher, and one thing led to another as it often does. On September 20, 1959, Eleanor became Mrs. John Biener. Shortly thereafter, on July 17, 1960, Sandi was born, followed by Rosine, Don, and Patricia. Children are a mixed blessing. They are wonderful and exciting and I loved coming home from work to see their shining, smiling faces. On the other hand, those shining, smiling faces like to be fed at least three times a day, and kids seem to outgrow their shoes every week. I'd gone from being a fairly carefree bachelor to a family man with some serious husband and daddy responsibilities. My bill collecting job churned up a lot more anxiety for me than money, so I needed to develop a new plan. Quickly.

Family to the rescue. My brother Tom's soon-to-be wife Patricia contacted her Uncle Charlie to see if he had a spot for a hardworking—and not particularly fussy—laborer. Charlie Yeagel was the manager of the Welding Swimming Pool Company in Hempstead, Long Island. The company was involved in all aspects of the home swimming pool business, from going out on the initial site surveys to finishing and cleaning new pools. Charlie gave me a job starting at the bottom, which was fair. In this case, however, the bottom really was the bottom. I'd be standing in the bottom of an unfinished swimming pool scooping out excess gunite with a long-handled shovel. Gunite is a concrete substance and heavy, particularly if all you have to move it is your own muscle. Grateful as I was for the job, the novelty of this grew old quickly. I was either going to have the world's strongest back or no back at all. To make things worse, the boss's brother had taken a dislike to me for some reason. When we'd go out on a site survey for a new pool installation he would mark the boundaries for the dig with wooden pegs that he would drive into the ground with a long-handled sledgehammer. Guess who got to hold the pegs? Every time we did that I was sweating bullets, waiting for the "accidental" miss that would shatter my right wrist.

One hot day I was shoveling away at the bottom of a pool when a chance for upward mobility (literally) presented itself. The foreman yelled down asking if anyone knew how to drive a dump truck. I immediately said I could do the job and climbed out of the hole. In fact, I knew nothing about driving a dump truck. The company had several trucks for different purposes, but all I knew about the dump truck was that I'd be gripping a steering wheel instead of a shovel. I was confident I could figure it out, so I jumped up into the cab, slipped it into gear, and headed off to the landfill where I needed to dump the load. So far, so good.

When I got to the landfill I could see the area where other trucks were dumping, so I positioned the truck over there. When I figured I was in the right spot I pulled the lever labeled "dump." It didn't. Instead it made a hellacious whining noise that sounded like the back end was trying to twist itself off of the frame. I climbed out of the cab to take a look and found a lever that looked like it might be the locking mechanism for the bucket. I pulled it, got back in the cab, and tried again. This time I could see the bucket rising, so I put the truck in gear and slowly let it roll forward. I'd seen guys dumping loads before, so I mimicked what they did. I drove forward a bit and occasionally tapped the brakes to jar the load loose. It worked. The truck was empty and I went back for another load.

I dumped several loads and I was on my second day of driving when I spotted one of the landfill workers heading my way. He drove the bulldozer that spread the dumped piles of debris out so that the land was flat again. He'd been watching me work from his perch on the 'dozer and was marching my way with a look on his face that indicated he had something on his mind and I was about to get a piece of it. I tensed up. To my surprise he said, "Hey, I like the way you're doing this stuff, but the other guy (referring to the other Welding dump truck driver), tell them to keep him at home." I took that as a professional endorsement. I was now an acknowledged professional dump truck driver.

While driving my truck through Syosset, Long Island, I'd passed a nightclub called The Oaks many times. A sign out front said they had live entertainment on Saturday nights. I knew I was pretty entertaining and I was certainly alive, so I figured maybe I could make a little money performing there. One Saturday night I put on my suit and headed to The Oaks to see if I could talk someone into giving me a try.

When I went through the front door, the place was pretty much what I expected. It was dimly lit through a haze of cigarette smoke laced with alcohol fumes. The bar was straight ahead of me with about six men and women perched on stools, and the entrance to the showroom was to my right. It was fifty feet wide by seventy-five feet deep with a small stage on the right side and about a dozen tables. There were twenty or so customers in the place and I got there just in time to see the comedian on stage finish his act. One guy applauded. It sounded like two fish being slapped together. The comic made a hasty escape and the musicians, a trio, played him off and then took a break.

As they walked past me I asked one of them who the club manager was. He pointed to a guy about six feet, four inches tall, sixtyish, in a dark suit. He was standing in the back of the room with his hands in his pockets, jingling change. If you can imagine Rodney Dangerfield as a club manager you've got the picture. He looked to be about as happy with the comic's performance as the audience had been. His name was Dick Metts. I introduced myself, told him I was a comic, and asked if I could get up on stage and try some things out. He nodded his head toward the quiet audience and without taking his hands out of his pockets said, "It couldn't hurt."

It couldn't hurt. Not a lot of enthusiasm there, but at least he didn't say no. I'd gotten past the indifferent club manager, but now I had to go up in front of the audience that hadn't been all that pleased with the previous act. They'd expected entertainment and they hadn't gotten it. I would have to win them over.

When they record a comedy TV show in Hollywood, they always hire a comedian to entertain the studio audience before they begin taping. This is called a "warm-up act." The purpose? Just that—to get the audience in a good mood, ready to laugh. Warmed up. The audience that I was about to step in front of was cold as ice and hungry for something entertaining. That was my job.

I hadn't really performed for more than a few people at a time since I'd gotten out of the navy, so I didn't have a well-rehearsed, polished act ready to go. Knowing I might be a little rough around the edges, I decided to build the whole set around my Ed Sullivan impression. I would get up on stage and go directly into Ed introducing celebrities like he did on his TV show, then I would do my impressions of them. I had a quick conversation with the trio before I went up to let them know what songs and singers I'd be doing, so they'd know what to play. The trio played a quick tune and then the bass player, Bob Dorian, introduced me. With that, I hopped on stage and went for it.

When you step into the spotlight in a dark nightclub it takes a little time for your eyes to adjust to the change in light. This was the one time that may have worked in my favor, since the last guy hadn't left a lot of smiling faces in the audience. I launched into my act and immediately got laughs. I heard the audience before I saw them. I did my Elvis and Johnny Mathis impressions with accompaniment from the trio, as well as an impression of President Kennedy as a football coach. ("Men," I said in his refined Boston accent, "I realize the situation doesn't look good and want you to know that when I agreed to play against these Texas Longhorns I had no idea we'd be playing against real steers.) I also did tough-guy actor John Wayne, with his distinctive voice and walk, as a priest. The audience loved it.

Dick Metts loved it, too. He loved it enough to offer me a three-month, Saturday night gig at The Oaks for forty dollars a night. It doesn't sound like much now after decades of inflation, but it was pretty decent money back then. And besides, how many part-time jobs are there where you get to be surrounded by laughter all night?

While I was working at The Oaks I brought on my friend, pianist Dean Christopher. Dean uses Christopher as a stage name, but his real last name is Calcagno. We worked really well together, and it was great to work with someone who always knew exactly what I was doing. Dean's father, newspaper cartoonist Joe Calcagno, became a big help during this time.

He introduced me to Irving Mansfield who was producing the Merv Griffin *Talent Scouts* show on TV. After an audition in Irving's office I was booked on to the show. The idea behind the Griffin show was that show business insiders would present new talent as their "find." Joe and Irving presented me on the show as their discovery.

After that show, every once in a while I'd get a shot at something bigger. The first one was great. I was booked into a nightclub in Washington, DC, called The Shadows working with the Ahmad Jamal Trio. The engagement was for two or three weeks. Dean was with me and we had a ball. After that I picked up a gig here and there, but I was still a far way from being a star. I ended up picking up a side job working at the gas station around the corner from our apartment to earn a few extra bucks to take care of the family. If someone tells you show business can be tough, believe them.

The presidency of John F. Kennedy was a gold mine for impressionists. He was handsome, cultured, and from a large, wealthy family that did interesting things like play touch football on the lawn of the family mansion. With his Bostonian accent and speech patterns he was an endless source of material. There got to be so many people impersonating JFK that a special Kennedy impersonation contest was held in Manhattan. I'd been riding the Kennedy wave myself for quite a while and I was pretty good at doing him, so off I went into the city to perform. Sitting in the audience that night was Vaughn Meader, the acknowledged king of the Kennedy impersonators. He'd earned a Gold Record and a Grammy Award with an album called "The First Family." If you turned on your radio during that period it was a safe bet you were going to hear a cut from the album. There were plenty of other industry insiders there that night, and the house was filled with comedy lovers. I scored big time, taking the first-place prize. I won ten dollars. It paid for my car fare.

One of the other comics in the club that night was a guy named Bob, who had a rubberlike face that he could contort for laughs. He came up to me after the contest and asked me if I'd like to join him in an improv.

"Sure, great, love to," I said. "What's an improv?" An improv, he explained to me, was going up on stage with just an idea for a situation and making up dialogue on the spot. The premise he came up with was that he would be the pilot of an airplane that couldn't get its wheels down and I would be the air traffic controller. We would improvise the radio conversation. I agreed to the whole thing, although I wasn't a hundred percent certain of what I was getting myself into.

Bob went up on stage, made a couple of faces, got a couple of laughs, and told the audience what we were about to do. He was piloting an airplane with no landing gear, I was the air traffic controller, and he was going to radio me for instructions. The audience was excited to see what would happen. So was I, but not necessarily in a good way. It would've been nice to have a little practice at this kind of thing and not have to try it out for the first time in front of an audience, but it was too late to back out now. Bob started the bit.

"Pilot to tower, pilot to tower. Request permission to land," he said. I drew a complete blank. I just stood there.

He tried again. "Pilot to tower, pilot to tower. Request permission to land." I still didn't have a clue what to say, so I just stood there silently. He tried again.

"Pilot to tower, pilot to tower. Request permission to land." I knew I had to say something this time and was starting to panic. Then all of a sudden it was like God handed me a line. The voice of Rod Steiger, known for his ability to slowly deliver a line and milk it for dramatic effect, leaped into my mind.

"Boooy, have I got neeews for yooou," I said in my Steiger voice. The audience came apart. The laugh was huge. I got off the stage while I was ahead.

It had been a great night for me and I was on top of the world. In the lobby there were people shaking my hand, congratulating me, and sticking their business cards in my face. One of those business cards belonged to a man named Harry Colomby. Harry said awkwardly, "Hey, I like you. You got this thing . . ." pointing to his throat. Harry and I went out for coffee and I found I liked him, too. Harry was actually a schoolteacher, but he loved show business and entertainers and he was trying to break in as a manager. He was basically making handshake deals. He didn't have a contract with his talent, just a mutual agreement that he would work on their behalf and he would get a percentage of whatever money he got for them. When I first met him he was representing two first-rate musical acts, Thelonious Monk and Mose Allison. I was his first comedian.

Harry had a pretty good sense of humor himself. He called me on the phone one day and told me he'd been at a party the previous night where he met impressionist Rich Little, famous for impersonating a number of celebrities on stage. "I walked up behind him and tapped him on the shoulder and no one was there," he said. On another night I was walking down the street with Harry and his wife, Lee, when she looked up at the insects buzzing around and asked, "Why do moths fly around the light?"

"Because they like to read," Harry responded.

Harry and I started with a handshake deal, that grew into a sixteen-year professional relationship. He started by taking advantage of his connections and clients in the music world. He booked me into jazz clubs where I would perform between musical acts. This actually worked out better than it might seem, because I had incorporated impersonations of musical artists like Tony Bennett, Nat King Cole, and Mel Tormé into my act. I brought my friend, pianist Dean Christopher, with me so my accompaniment was always perfect.

One of my favorite bits was on Frank Sinatra. I set up the impersonation by saying that Sinatra was so good it didn't even matter what he was singing about—anything that came out of his mouth sounded like a love song. I'd then ask the audience to come up with any topic, and I'd improvise Sinatra turning it into a love song. One night a guy in the audience yelled out, "Linoleum." Dean started to play a melody that sounded like a Sinatra love song, and I started throwing out lyrics off the top of my head:

"I think of you when I look at my linoleum,
It reminds me of your face,
Some blue, some green, some in between,
An occasional scuff mark or two.
Baby that's you."

With Harry's foot in the door I slipped into some of the hottest jazz clubs in New York. In addition to my gig at the Village Vanguard I frequently performed at the Five Spot and did a memorable one-nighter at the Blue Angel with John Coltrane. I was getting pretty good at coming up with lyrics spontaneously, and Dean was always there with the right melody, so we were putting on a pretty good show. It looked like I had a promising career as a New York club comic.

And then Jack Babb walked into the Vanguard.

# Chapter Four

## *A Really Big Show*

And this is where we came in. March 1, 1964, when Jack Babb walked into my dressing room at *The Ed Sullivan Show* as I was preparing to go home and told me that "the boss" liked me, and oh, by the way, I'm going on live TV in a couple of hours in front of millions of people. Surprise!

Obviously, this was another of those good news, bad news situations. The good news—and it was overwhelmingly good—was that I was going to be on *The Ed Sullivan Show*. The bad news was that in my wildest dreams I never thought it would be that night. I'd gone out of "performance mode" after the audition and slipped back into "relaxation mode." I now had to gear up for another performance, and this one much more important than the first.

If you ever saw Ed Sullivan on TV you couldn't forget him. If you are too young to have seen him it's worth a couple of minutes to paint the picture for you. He was a New York City native, born in Harlem in 1901, of Irish descent. He'd had a very successful career as a newspaperman, first as a sportswriter and then a Broadway columnist, but being close to the spotlight wasn't good enough for Ed. He wanted to be in it. He used his newspaper celebrity status to launch a side career producing vaudeville shows in the '20s and '30s and cast himself as the master of ceremonies. He replicated this format first in radio and, in 1948, on CBS television. The show was originally called *Toast of the Town*, but was soon renamed

*The Ed Sullivan Show*. His distinctive TV persona made him an entertainment commodity as much as his guests. This may not seem unusual unless you know that Ed was probably the most unlikely show business host of that or any other era. In fact, one TV critic said, "He got where he is not by having a personality, but by having no personality." That was kind of a nasty barb, and was intended to be so, but it wasn't at all true. In fact, Ed probably had as much or more personality as anyone else on the air. It was just different. Really different.

First, there were Ed's looks. He had been a good-looking young man in his early newspaper days, and was still good-looking when I first met him in his early sixties. It was his body and movements that made him unique. For openers, he looked like he had been starched into his suit. His movements were stiff and robotic. It seemed like he didn't have a neck. He had a tendency to turn his whole body from the waist rather than just turn his head. He even seemed a little stiff when he applauded the acts on his stage, but his smile was genuine.

Second, he had a way of speaking that they don't teach in broadcasting schools. It was slightly nasal and he spoke in short, clipped sentences. Some of his catchphrases became part of the American culture, such as "Right here, on our stage . . ." and "Tonight we have a really big show." In addition to occasionally mangling the English language, he would also sometimes mess up the introductions of his acts. One night he introduced the Three Stooges as the Three Ritz Brothers. Jim Henson's Muppets became Jim Newsom's Puppets. One night he wanted to send a personal greeting to his son-in-law, Bob Precht, who was ill. Unfortunately, it came out "My son-in-law, Bob Hope, is ill and we all hope he's feeling better soon." He once introduced Diana Ross and The Supremes as "Three black girls from Detroit." But it's important to understand that Ed never meant to be rude or demeaning. He just had a tendency to be forgetful and jumble his words. In fact, The Supremes was one of Ed's favorite acts and made seventeen appearances on his show. He always referred to the group affectionately as "The Girls," although Diana Ross, who apparently liked Ed a lot, once joked that she thought he may have called them that because he couldn't remember their names.

Sometimes Ed would think one of his mistakes was funny enough to repeat, but even that wasn't foolproof. My friend Jack Jones was making his first appearance on Ed's show and during the dress rehearsal Ed asked him, "Wasn't your father Allan Jones?" Since Allan Jones was still very much alive Jack responded, "He still is." The audience broke up laughing, so Ed decided they would do it the same way in the live broadcast. The show went on and Jack was ready with his snappy response when Ed asked, "*Isn't* your father Allan Jones?" Well, yes . . .

As you can imagine, a guy like Ed was a dream come true for a guy like me. I, along with my fellow professional impressionists and thousands of amateurs in living rooms across America, had a field day doing Ed. There were dozens of "Sullivanisms" that worked their way into American culture that didn't actually come from Ed. ("Right here, on our stage, the entire original cast of World War Two.") Rather than be insulted by the shots at his fumbles, Ed loved them. He had a great sense of humor about himself and enjoyed these send-ups as much as the audience. Maybe more.

Ed was a publicist's dream, too. One of the unique features of his show was to introduce celebrities who were seated in the studio audience. A celebrity passing through New York could get some major network exposure by doing nothing more than sitting in Ed's audience. Ed would announce, "Joining us tonight in our studio audience is the world renown . . ." and then the actor/ musician/athlete, whatever they might be, stood up, acknowledged the audience applause, and sat down. If they had a new film or record album coming out, Ed plugged it. If not, they got their face and name on TV before millions anyway. That was it. Thirty seconds and done.

Even these brief cameos weren't foolproof in the hands (and mouth) of Ed. One night a Broadway star was the inadvertent victim when Ed introduced her: "In our audience tonight, a star who is now *starving* on Broadway in *Destry Rides Again*, Dolores Gray." The "starving" Miss Gray rose and accepted her applause as Ed caught his mistake. "You don't look like you're starving," he laughed as he waved.

The audience accepted this as part of his strange charm and loved it. It could get kind of exciting for the performer, though. What Ed said he was going to do in rehearsal and what he did on the show were not necessarily the same thing. You had to stay on your toes.

There's one thing about Ed that is undisputed: he loved talent and he didn't discriminate. At a time when African-American performers had a hard time getting on TV, Ed was colorblind. If you were good, you were on. Plain and simple. Ed was conservative with what he considered to be high moral values. When the rock 'n' roll wave broke, Ed was concerned about the gyrations of the performers and some of the lyrics in the new genre. He was leery of Elvis Presley, but put him on the show anyway, later stating that he thought he was a fine young man. The fact that Elvis's appearance drew 60 million viewers—over 82 percent of the television audience at that time—was certainly a nice bonus for taking the risk. The Rolling Stones, the Doors, and several other rock 'n' roll acts were instructed to change lyrics that Ed found too suggestive. The ones that complied stood a good chance of getting rebooked. The ones who didn't were shunned. That's the way it went with Ed. It was his show and he ran it the way he wanted to. If you did it his way everything was fine. If you crossed him he had a short temper and a long memory.

The fact that Ed could, and did, do anything he wanted to worked in my favor that night. Since it was a live broadcast, the timing of the show had to be 100 percent perfect. There was no such thing as editing out mistakes and timing errors later. The director and production crew had to end the show at the exact second dictated by the network schedule. That meant that every performer on the show had been given a specific amount of time for their act and had planned and rehearsed it to fit. The production staff had created a rundown and format with times indicated so they would know exactly where they were at every moment during the broadcast and ensure that they would end on time. The scheduling and timing process had been discussed and planned for days. No one would intentionally make a last-minute schedule change. No one except Ed. Ed wanted me on the show that night, and that's the way it was going to be. The other performers were told they were having their time cut to make room for me and raced to rework their acts to fit the new schedule. The production crew had to create new rundowns and get them distributed to the crew. If you wanted to screw up a live network TV show at the last minute, this would be a fine way to do it. Plunging me into the show had created some seriously big ripples in a lot of people's evenings.

I had to cut my act as well. Like everyone else, the set I'd done at the dress rehearsal was now too long for the show. Jack told me to cut my Dean Martin bit. Everyone got busy shaving seconds off their act and hoped the whole thing would work in the end.

I got to a telephone as quickly as I could to tell my mother I was going to be on the show. "Which half?" she said. She was excited and wanted to call all of her friends but she didn't want them to have to watch the entire show if they didn't want to, just the part with me in it. She was very considerate that way. It made me laugh.

The first order of business was going downstairs to wardrobe to get my suit pressed. I only had one suit and I'd worn it for the dress rehearsal, so it was slightly wrinkled during the drive from Long Island. They also took my shoes to give them another shine. They gave me a robe and a pair of flip-flops to wear while they worked on my clothes. The wardrobe department was on the floor below the stage. I decided to wait for my clothes in my dressing room, which meant I had to walk down a hallway that ran directly beneath the stage to the staircase that would take me back upstairs. As I started up the stairs one of the flip-flops slipped and I almost fell. I heard a voice from the top of the stairway say, "I hope you break your neck." I looked up and saw comedian Jack Carter sitting on a folding chair next to the elevator, apparently waiting for me. He was also on the show that night and had time cut out of his act to make room for me. He obviously wasn't very happy about it and wanted me to know it.

My debut on *The Ed Sullivan Show* was typical of the way Ed liked to present a variety of entertainment. In addition to the unhappy Jack Carter—who took a few cynical shots at the recent appearance by The Beatles—I shared the bill with Hollywood movie star George Raft, who danced the tango with The Hugh Lambert Dancers. Pop artists The Barry Sisters sang, as did gospel singer Russell Newport, and in keeping with Ed's "something for everyone" philosophy, ventriloquist Rickie Layne and Velvel did a Beatles-themed set. But wait . . . there's more! The Alcettys balanced wine glasses and a lamp on a spinning platter, and The Longbunny Sisters rounded out the hour by tossing flaming batons. I think it's safe to say that if you didn't see it on *The Ed Sullivan Show*, it probably didn't exist. At a time when most Americans only had one television set, it was a pretty smart way to put a show together.

I took the elevator up to my dressing room on the third floor where Harry was waiting for me. We went over my act again and in a little while the wardrobe people delivered my clothes. After I got dressed it was close enough to show time to head down to the stage. There, for the first time, I met Ed Sullivan. He extended his hand and gave me a smile.

"Hi there, youngster. Where are you from?"

"Baldwin," I replied, knowing that he'd be familiar with the Long Island community. We had a couple of minutes of pleasant conversation, but not much more. It was show time. I was nervous and excited and much of my memory of those moments is hazy, but I distinctly remember Ed giving me my introduction.

"And now, here's a young comic from Baltimore, John Byner!"

*Baltimore?*

I stepped onto the stage, went into my act, and got laughs immediately. The worst thing a comedian can hear is the sound of silence, so that was a big relief. As I moved through my act I could tell that I was going over really well, but my tension never fully went away. I got a big round of applause after my last bit, took a quick bow, and headed over to Ed. He always stayed stage right as the acts performed, and the performers would walk over to him for a handshake and a personal word when they completed their set. Ed had a big grin on his face as I shook his hand, but when I turned to get off stage he didn't let go. Instead, he turned to the audience and said, "Do you want to hear him do Dean Martin?" The Dean Martin bit had been cut for time, but I guess Ed didn't care about time anymore. He completely caught me—and Ray Bloch and the orchestra—off guard. I went into a few bars of Dean singing "An Evening in Roma," and Ray and the orchestra, by some miracle, were right with me. I was so surprised and nervous that my Dean Martin sounded a little more like Jerry Lewis, but Ed and the audience loved it. I walked off stage feeling tremendous relief and excitement. Then I spent the next couple of days explaining to my friends in Baldwin why Ed said I was from Baltimore.

Ed liked me. I was always very happy about that because I liked him. And, from purely a business angle, *The Ed Sullivan Show* was a big boost for my career. I would do the show on a Sunday night and the next week, somewhere on the road, I would see my name on the marquee with the words, "Direct from *The Ed Sullivan Show.*" Those words were a big deal.

I ended up making seventeen appearances on *The Ed Sullivan Show* and most—probably all—had a Sullivan impersonation in them. I loved it, the audience loved it, and Ed loved it, so why not? In fact, sometimes Ed liked a bit so much he wanted to get involved. I had an idea for a bit in which Ed's show was pre-empted by a news event and he only had ten minutes to get in all of his guests. I would impersonate Ed as well as all of the acts as he raced to get through the show. I rehearsed it for Ed, and it went like this:

I opened with Ed introducing Frank Sinatra: "And now, right here on our stage . . ." etc.

Me, as Frank Sinatra singing "A Very Good Year": "When I was seventeen, I . . ."

Me, as Ed, interrupting: "Hold it, Frank! Is this going to go seventeen, eighteen, nineteen? We'll be here all night. You come back on our Easter Show and finish that. Now folks, we were going to have the juggling Barzoni Brothers on the show tonight, but we only have time for one brother. Take it away."

Me, as a bewildered Barzoni Brother with an Italian accent: "It's-a not the same-a without my brother."

He picks up the juggling pins and tosses them across the stage where they crash into the curtain and onto the floor. He then runs over to a seesaw where he jumps on one side to vault his missing brother into the air, then pantomimes catching him. Finally, he runs toward the camera in frustration.

Me, as a Barzoni Brother: "See . . . I come-a a several thousand miles to catch-a nothing!"

Me, as Ed: "Just fine . . . just fine simulated catch. And now, here's my little friend, Topo Gigio." (Topo Gigio was a puppet that would have conversations with Ed while sitting in the palm of Ed's hand..)

Topo cuddles up to Ed's face.

Me, as Topo Gigio with an Italian accent: "Hello Eddy. Keeze me good nighht."

Me, as Ed: "Here's your kiss, Topo." (Kisses him) "We don't have much time, so let's hear it for Topo Gigio!"

Ed forgets Topo is a puppet and Topo goes flying across the stage when Ed claps.

I had several more famous people in the bit when I ran it for Ed and he loved it. He wanted to give me a special introduction that set up the premise. In rehearsal he was great. He stepped out to center stage with me and said, "I understand you are going to show us what the show would look like if we only had ten minutes," and I responded, "Right." "Okay, go ahead and do it," he said with a smile as he walked back to his spot on stage right.

On the live show, in front of millions of people, it didn't go quite that well. He introduced me, "And now, here's comedian John Byner." I walked to my spot next to him, waiting for his setup, and he said nothing. Finally he said, "Well do it!" and walked away. I turned to the audience and said, "What Ed means to say is . . ." and explained the bit. The bit became something of a classic. To this day I'll be walking through an airport or hotel somewhere when I'll hear someone shout out, "It's not the same without my brother!"

Sometimes life imitates art rather than the other way around. Something like "The Ten Minute Ed Sullivan Bit" actually happened once and I was on the show. That was part of the thrill of live TV; things could happen that blew up everyone's carefully laid plans. It was October 18, 1964, and I was booked onto the Sullivan show with Van Johnson, Rita Pavone, Joan Sutherland, Jackie Mason, and Eric Burdon and the Animals. The show was planned in the usual format, but President Lyndon Johnson's White House threw us a curve. They announced that LBJ was going to give a special speech on Russia and nuclear weapons, so CBS had to carry it. The speech would last thirty minutes and preempt the second half of *The Ed Sullivan Show*. I was fortunate to be booked on the first half hour, so I knew I was going to perform, but that didn't spare me from a strange evening.

The year 1964 was the beginning of what came to be known as the British Music Invasion. It had begun earlier in the year with The Beatles, and a number of British acts with the British sound quickly followed. Ed was open to booking the new acts, but they brought something with them other than music. Their fans, particularly young girls, tended to scream, jump around, and generally cause quite a commotion in the theater, but this was all part of the overall scene.

When the shortened show opened with Eric Burdon and the Animals, the expected ruckus involved the audience acting like . . . well, sort of like animals. Ed had to calm the audience down so they could perform their second song. After that Ed interviewed a couple of baseball players, Van Johnson and Rita Pavone appeared, and I went on to a nice, receptive audience. So far, so good. We made it to the half hour point and the network cut away for LBJ's speech.

Normally I would head back to my dressing room after my set, but if the president felt he had to interrupt programming on a Sunday night to say something, I figured I should stay around and listen. The theater had monitors in it where the audience could see the telecast as well as the acts on stage, but now these monitors were tuned to the speech. I sat in the theater and, with everyone else, waited to see what kind of drama the nation was in for. Johnson spoke about a power shake-up in Russia (Cold War bogeyman Nikita Khrushchev had been bumped out of power by Alexei Kosygin, an unknown quantity) and the Chinese had detonated a nuclear bomb. This was not the ideal way to polish off an evening of light entertainment, but there was nothing we could do about that.

Life happens and LBJ had the floor for thirty minutes. Then something else interesting happened. He stopped talking.

It seems that the half hour speech announced by the White House was only eighteen-and-a-half minutes long. The CBS network would be cutting back to the Sullivan show, which meant, naturally, that there actually had to be a show going on. While newsman Martin Kalb did a wrap up of Johnson's speech, the Sullivan staff and crew leaped into action. They didn't yet know how much time would be left for the show and they couldn't accurately calculate it until they were back on the air. All they really could do was get the next act, Jackie Mason, on stage and figure it out while he was doing his set in front of millions of people. Not great.

Kalb talked for about three minutes and then CBS threw it to us, and Jackie was on the air. This is when another little problem turned up. The young audience who had shown up to see the Animals, who were bookending the show, had gotten restless during the speech. They wanted the band back on stage—and only the band. Jackie was having a tough time getting laughs. He was even getting some light heckling. At one point he told them in frustration, "I've told you thirty jokes; pick one you like."

Meanwhile, back in the control room, they'd figured out exactly how much time they had left in the show and they needed to let everyone else know. I had done about six minutes that night, which was probably about what Jackie was originally scheduled for, but now they needed to cut his time to get the last act on. Ed apparently got a two-minute cue, so he waved two fingers at Jackie. Then he told the stage manager to get behind the camera to be ready to give him the one-minute cue.

At this point Jackie was starting to score. He was doing

a bit about married actors Richard Burton and Elizabeth Taylor, whose Hollywood/storybook/tumultuous marriage kept them in the news and had recently earned them the cover of *LIFE* magazine. Jackie, in his New York Jewish accent, was analyzing the couple and the audience was loving it. ("Richard Boyton is always talking about Lizbit Talah, Lizbit dis, Lizbit dat . . . you never hear me talk about huh!") As the audience laughed the stage manager raised his finger for the one-minute cue. Jackie responded, "Look at dis! I'm gettin' hot and they're given me da finger! Well, here's a finger for you (toward the band), a finger for you (toward the audience), and a finger for you (toward Ed)." With that he stormed off stage left. Jackie's hands were outside the camera shot, so the TV audience couldn't see his fingers, but when the camera cut to Ed it was pretty clear what had just happened. It was one of those "if looks could kill" moments.

Ed held it together long enough to get Eric Burdon and the Animals back on stage to sing "The House of the Rising Sun," and then filled out the hour with a tribute to Cole Porter, who had died earlier that week, and a plug about an upcoming Rolling Stones appearance. I headed up to my dressing room to take off my makeup and change clothes for the drive home. I always walked past Ed's dressing room on my way out to say good night to him and whoever else might be there. Ed's door was always open . . . except for that night.

Ed's voice came through the closed door like a chainsaw. He was letting Jackie know, in the harshest of street language, how he felt about Jackie's actions. I'd heard plenty of new words in the navy, but Ed was charting new territory. The part I can print went something like, "I've got kids, nuns, priests, and rabbis watching this show and you do something like *that*!" I actually lingered there for a few moments, kind of stunned by the whole thing. Every once in a while I heard Jackie say, "But, Ed . . ." As far as I know Jackie never finished a sentence.

But back to the fun stuff . . .

A couple of years later I was doing an impression of Tony Bennett performing on the Sullivan show. I was impersonating both Ed, with his heavy New York accent, as well as Tony. In Ed's introduction I had him mentioning that Tony was coming direct from a performance at the famous Copa Cabana nightclub.

Me, as Ed: "Now, direct from the Cope-er, here's Tony Bennett."

Me, as Tony singing: "I want to be around to pick up the pieces . . ."

Suddenly Ed interrupted me and stepped out to center stage. "Hold it, Byner, I don't say Cope-er, I say Copa. Now do it right." He then turned and headed back to his stage-right spot. I didn't see that coming, but I recovered quickly.

Me, as Ed: "And now, direct from the Co-Pa . . ." I said it very carefully and deliberately, pronouncing each syllable as I looked his way. Ed turned and nodded his head in agreement, ". . . Cabban-er," I continued. The audience completely lost it. The laughs were long and hard and Ed loved it.

In addition to everything else, Ed was a man's man and enjoyed having a laugh with—or at the expense of—the guys. Shortly after I did my first Sullivan show, Ed invited me to be in a stage show he was doing at Harrah's in Lake Tahoe,

Nevada. It was basically going to be the same format as his TV show, only without the cameras. I was to appear with comedian Bob King, impressionist Marilyn Michaels, a trained dog act called Berger's Animals, and Olympic-medal-winning gymnast Dick Albers, who did a trampoline act. Good show, nice people, great gig. One evening I was chatting up one of the long-legged showgirls when a pair of arms squeezed me from behind and I heard Ed say, "Don't listen to a word this red-headed son of a bitch tells you." He caught me completely by surprise and the three of us broke up laughing.

One afternoon during the Tahoe run I had some free time and decided to go to my dressing room and put another shine on my shoes. My dressing room was right across the hall from Ed's and I could hear that he and Jack Babb were in there having a conversation. I didn't want to interrupt, so I just went into my room and went to work. I was in a pretty good mood. Things were going great and I was a happy guy. As I buffed my shoes I began to whistle. I hadn't been in show business long enough to know that there was a superstition about whistling in a dressing room and it just isn't done. Ed was about to explain it to me.

"Who's that whistling over there?" I heard him ask, quietly.

"It's Byner, Ed," Jack Babb answered.

Ed's voice rose, loud enough to be heard throughout the dressing room area. "Byner, don't you know it's taboo to whistle in a dressing room?" he shouted. I'd never heard of that before, so I said nothing. After a long pause he shouted, "One more peep out of you and I'll come over there and string you up by your red balls!," followed by muffled laugher from him and Jack.

It's interesting to look back on the Sullivan shows I did after all these years. Time adds a new perspective. I knew

I was performing on a top network show and I knew I was performing with others who were at the top of their game, but it didn't seem like history-making stuff at the time. Now, when I look at those cast lists and see names like The Beatles, The Mamas and the Papas, and Joe Cocker and the Grease Band, it's obvious that I was right in the middle of a major cultural revolution. Ed bridged the generation gap with performances by Ray Milland and Van Johnson to teen idols Annette Funicello and Frankie Avalon. I can't remember any show exactly like *The Ed Sullivan Show*, and it's unlikely there will ever be anything like it again. He had America's eyes and ears for twenty-three years.

Ed Sullivan was a unique man whose talent was spotting talent. I'm glad to have had him as a friend.

# Chapter Five

## *Rolling, Rolling, Rolling*

Being a comedian doesn't bear much resemblance to a normal job, unless you're a traveling salesman. It's not like having a store or an office where your customers come to you; you have to go to them. The process is pretty much the same today as it was when I started. This is another one of those good news-bad news deals. It's great if you like to go to new places and meet new people. It's not so great if you like sleeping in your own bed and seeing your family on a regular basis, but it's part of the deal if you want a few laughs and a decent paycheck. It's always been fine with me.

I'd done pretty well on the Merv Griffin *Talent Scouts* show, which got me some attention. It also got me my first road gig in Rochester, New York. It wasn't exactly Chicago or Hollywood, but it was my first out-of-town booking and that was a big deal. I packed up my car and drove the 362 miles upstate from Baldwin to where I had been booked to perform for two weeks in a two-bay gas station. Actually, it was a former corner gas station that three guys had converted into a coffee shop. They'd removed the gas pumps to create a parking lot and erected a small stage between the service bays, but let's face it, there's only so much you can do to a gas station to make it not look like a gas station. It was fine with me, though. The three owners were good guys, there was an audience and money. Good enough for me.

Performing in a converted gas station in Rochester on

cold, snowy winter evenings comes with its own challenges. To fend off the chill, the owners had installed a salamander oil heater about four feet in front of the stage with a large chimney right in the sight line of the audience. Since it was a coffee shop they had to have coffee, so they had installed an espresso machine in what had once been the gas station office. Every time they made a cup of espresso the final blast of steam sounded like the release of air brakes on a semi-truck, and it always seemed to drop right on top of my punchline. Despite all of this I had a great time and the two weeks flew by.

The owners had excellent taste in picking talent, if I do say so myself. Between my sets a young horn player, a guy I knew only as Chuck, performed. He was really good and the crowd and I loved him. A few years later I was in the car with my jazz-buff manager, Harry, and we were listening to a great horn player on the radio. "That's Chuck," Harry said, "the guy you performed with in the gas station. Chuck Mangione." Who knew? Unfortunately, I've never run into him since that gig so long ago, but he's really taken off in the music world and I'm happy about that. He's a talented guy and always was.

I stayed in touch with the coffee shop owners for several years, but I eventually lost contact with them. I've always wondered how long the place lasted and where they are now. I heard that one of them had gone into the car repossession business and told the story about being hit in the back of the head with a brick as he tried to escape with a repo. That story makes comedy seem a whole lot easier. I reached a milestone in 1964 when I received my American Federation of Television and Radio Artists card. I was then officially recognized as a professional. Being recognized as a professional and actually working, however, are two different things. I found myself doing big shows with great people, only to have to take jobs pumping gas between gigs to feed my family. If you could get whiplash from abrupt job changes, I would have had it.

This schizophrenic career went on for a couple more years, but I was young and could take it. My performance life was going very well. I was getting enough attention that it made sense to add an agent to work with my manager. I became a client of the Agency for the Performing Arts (APA) represented by Don Gregory, and they quickly packaged me in with a tour they were building around Harry James and His Orchestra. Buddy Rich was the featured drummer and Nina Simone was the headlining vocalist. The band's regular vocalist, Ruth Price, was also on the tour. We would start on September 18, 1964, performing in New York City at the World's Fair Grounds, be on the road for twenty-seven days, and finish off in Omaha, Nebraska, on October 11 at the Sheridan Frontier. Since I'd only been in the business as a card-carrying entertainer for five or six months, this was a pretty big step up for me.

Harry Colomby drove me to the place where the band bus was to depart and we said goodbye. I was the last to arrive and as I started up the bus steps I was greeted by Harry James. He was seated in the second row behind the driver's seat, directly behind the lovely singer Ruth Price, whom I hadn't yet met. Ruth had her own accompaniment of sorts: a miniature dachshund was curled up comfortably on her lap.

"Hi Reds," he said, pronouncing it with an "s." Like most red-haired people, I'd been called Red from time to time my whole life, so I figured he had to be talking to me. I returned the greeting. "Are you married?" he asked. I told him I was, but I thought that was kind of an odd first question to ask. It occurred to me later that that question may have been for the benefit of Ruth. He gave me a big smile, and we were soon on our way. We had assigned seats on the bus and I was fortunate to sit next to saxophone player Jay Corey. He'd played with Harry for a long time, but he was also a much-in-demand session player on albums for a number of top musical acts. More importantly to me at that particular moment was that Jay was a really neat guy and I enjoyed talking to him. He had an infectious, guttural laugh, and spent plenty of time doing it. He became a combination of a traveling companion and encyclopedia of the world of music. I could not have chosen a better bus companion than Jay to sit next to for all of those hours. We kept in touch for many, many years after that tour.

The towns on the tour were all within driving distance, so that's how we traveled—some long trips, some short. Moving an entire orchestra by air every day would've cost a fortune, so that wasn't even an option, although Harry James and Ruth Price would take a plane if the cities were too far apart. Most of us rode on the tour bus, but Nina Simone traveled in a limousine with her quartet, preceded by a van with their instruments and luggage. Buddy Rich had a vehicle more in keeping with his own personal style. He drove his brand-new 1964 British racing green Jaguar fastback coupe, and he drove it hard. We'd hear someone in the back of the bus say, "Here comes Buddy," then there would be a roar from the Jaguar's exhaust and he'd pass us like we were standing still as he made for the horizon. "There goes Buddy."

Jazz and jazz musicians have been a big part of my life. They were the source of some of my more popular impressions, and I also spent much of my early career working in jazz clubs. That being said, some of them seem to live in a different world than the rest of us. I don't mean that in a bad way; they're just a little different. I didn't fully appreciate this until I hit the road with them. We generally traveled at night and I was never able to sleep on the bus. There were a few others with the same problem, so we'd gather together in a section of the bus and talk quietly about various things as the miles rolled by. One night trombone player Ray Sims, brother of sax player Zoot Sims, was telling stories about his father. He seemed to idolize the man and told story after story, most of which were pretty darn funny, about things his father had said and done. He had a flask of something or other tucked away, as did some of the other guys, and that seemed to make everything even funnier. He finished talking after a while and the laughter subsided. Ray drifted off to sleep, as did many of the guys, and it got quiet. A few minutes later, Ray awoke and blurted out, "Let's go dig him up!" to a huge laugh.

Another night we were rolling across the country and I was having a quick conversation with Jay. I'd been telling him about some of my experiences in the navy, particularly about having visited some of the big battle sites of the Pacific Theater in World War II. The conversation sort of ebbed and flowed. After a brief quiet spell I said, "I was on Kwajalein for a few months." One of the guys seated behind us apparently hadn't heard the entire conversation. "Man, you were on Kwajalein? How did you kick it?" I had to explain to him that Kwajalein was an island, not a drug.

The bus driver on this tour was a guy named Red Brown. He'd driven the bus for Harry James for years for two very good reasons. First, he was a good driver. He bragged that in all the time that he'd driven the band he'd never had to slam on the brakes once. That's kind of important. Nobody wants to be awakened from a sound sleep by being vaulted down the aisle of a bus on your face in the middle of the night by sloppy driving.

It was Red's other quality, however, that likely endeared him to the band. He was just as crazy as they were. My assigned seat on the bus was just three rows behind Red, so I didn't miss anything he said or did. Red was a pretty entertaining guy in his own right. One day we were out on the prairie driving, and driving, and driving. This was back in the days before interstate highways, of course, so we were riding that two-lane strip of asphalt through a seemingly endless world of nothing. There were no homes, no buildings, and not a whole lot of cars. Suddenly, on the horizon, Red spotted the roof of some kind of structure. As we got closer we could see that it was a tiny café out in the middle of nowhere.

Red saw an opportunity to break up the monotony of the road. He slowed the bus down and pulled up in front of the café, which looked like it had a counter with four stools and maybe two tables. The place probably didn't have more than a dozen customers a day. When the owner saw the full bus pull up he stepped outside with a look on his face that said, "How the hell am I going to feed all these people?" When it looked like the owner's mouth had dropped open as far as it could go, Red slipped the bus back into gear and off we went in a cloud of dust. We had a laugh, but the owner was probably happy to see us leave.

Another night we were somewhere out in the desert driving through a bleak terrain of nothing mixed with darkness. Occasionally a set of headlights would pass us in the other lane, but for the most part, there was nothing but the dull drone of the bus engine and the tires rolling over the asphalt. Even the most sleep-resistant among us had managed to drop off, except for me and I was 100 percent wide awake. From my seat three rows back I could see Red's face in the large rearview mirror. We rolled on and on and on and I suddenly noticed his head start to tilt forward. I thought he was checking something under the dash, but when it happened again I got concerned. In the mirror I saw his eyelids slowly start to close and his head began to slump forward again, then he straightened up quickly with a start. *Geez . . . he's falling asleep*, I thought. *All these guys on the bus trusting him with our lives, and he's falling asleep!* It happened again and my heart was in my throat. As I jumped up out of my seat to save us he straightened up, smiled at me in the mirror, and whispered, "Gotcha!" Ha, ha. Funny guy.

On the Harry James tour I was "the kid." There may have been a couple of horn players close to my age, but for the most part, I was a young and naïve guy surrounded by a mature and very worldly group of guys. Every business and company generally has someone who's "the kid." This has advantages as well as disadvantages. The older, more experienced guys will look out for you, but they also generally won't pass up an opportunity to give you a good ribbing.

I overslept one morning and the tour bus left without me. This is never good under any circumstances, but it's worse when you're "the kid." By the time I got it together, the bus had been gone for about twenty minutes. Fortunately, the hotel doorman offered to drive me to the bus in his car. He drove like a mad man and it wasn't too long until we caught up with the lumbering bus. My next problem was facing the band. When I got on board I was greeted with cheers, jeers, and applause. My seat mate, Jay Corey, knowing I'd eventually rejoin the band, had fashioned a dunce cap from sheet music and I was required to wear it for two hours. I didn't miss the bus again.

My job on the tour was to do my comedy act and then act as
a master of ceremonies for the rest of the show. The audiences
were generally really good as you would expect, since they
paid money for the tickets, but occasionally something
unusual would happen. One night in Massachusetts we had
an audience that was particularly talkative. It may have
been a group booking where everyone knew each other, but
whatever the deal was, they decided they wanted to talk
among themselves. There was quite a hubbub going on. There
was no curtain in the theater, so the acts entered and left the
stage in view of the audience. As Nina Simone swept onto
the stage into the spotlight next to the piano, I began to go
into her introduction, but the audience just kept on talking.
Nina told me to wait, so we both stood there silently in our
spotlights.

After a minute I tried to introduce her again and she said,
"Not yet." This happened several times and the audience was
showing no signs of shutting up. This was very disrespectful
to Nina and certainly uncomfortable for me. I waited until I
couldn't stand it anymore, then I gave it another try. "Ladies
and gentlemen . . ." I began, but that's as far as I got. I heard
Nina's voice with a distinct edge to it. "Don't open your
goddamned mouth until I'm ready!" She couldn't have been
much clearer on that; I got the message. So there we were,
me, Nina, and her quartet in our spotlights doing absolutely
nothing while the audience chattered away. Finally, they
figured out there was a show going on, or maybe they ran out
of things to talk about, but they quieted down and Nina went
into her set.

The thing I remember most about Nina was her impact
on an audience. When she sang, the world listened. She
seemed to cast a spell over the audience. Even the group in

Massachusetts fell under it. Once she started to sing you could hear a pin drop in the theater. The only sound was her beautiful voice. I had many pleasant conversations with Nina. She often spoke of her husband, and she introduced him to me a few years later when I ran into them at JFK Airport. She was a fine and talented lady.

I had less contact with Buddy Rich on that tour. The big names in the music industry tend to be vocalists, and I think it's fair to say that drummers get slighted a bit in the publicity area. Not so with Buddy. He and Gene Krupa stood apart from the rest in the mid-1900s and were household names. Buddy would stick around and talk for a while after the shows, but he seemed to like to be on his own. He'd climb into his Jag and blast out onto the highway and we frequently wouldn't see him again until we got to the next town where he would be waiting for us.

I ran into him a few years later when I was living in Malibu. He and his group were performing at Pepperdine University and I went to see him. The show was great, and Buddy invited me backstage when it was over. I sat through the post-show meeting he had with the band —where they discuss fixes and changes—then he and I went off to talk over old times. Buddy could be volatile, too. There is a great recording floating around of Buddy lecturing his band. It was in the early '60s and Buddy wasn't all that thrilled with the long-haired look they'd adopted. He went on and on about them looking like their mothers and the whole monologue is hilarious. I wish I could insert that tape into this book.

Harry James was good to me and I liked him. Every night he and Nina would do a little post-performance debriefing, frequently in the venue parking lot. They'd discuss the human factor in entertainment: the relationship of the performer and the audience. I found that fascinating and was able to listen in because I was with Harry. He always invited me to ride with him in the taxi back to the hotel, so I wasn't going anywhere until he did. He was a real pro and a gracious man. I wondered about one thing, however. In the cab, at some point he would put his hand over his mouth and fumble with something and then put his hand in his jacket pocket. I began to wonder if maybe he had a special set of false teeth or a bridge that he used specifically when he played his horn. Just another interesting little curiosity.

If someone in show business is unpleasant, word usually gets out. Gossip columnists used to have a field day with that kind of thing, and the tabloids do it today. You never heard or read anything bad about Harry James. The guys in his band respected him as a musician and a friend and genuinely liked him. Harry and his wife, Betty Grable, used to send me Christmas cards and I saved one. I break it out each year around the holidays and remember that great couple.

Carnegie Hall is one of the most famous performance venues in the United States and is known throughout the world. Steel gazillionaire Andrew Carnegie built the place at 57th Street and 7th Avenue in New York City in 1891, and ever since then a performance at Carnegie Hall is a career milestone for any entertainer. The Harry James tour was booked there, so this was a pretty significant event for me in my new line of work. I was walking through the dressing room area before the show and I heard the voice of the tour manager, Frank "Pee-Wee" Monte, complaining from Harry's dressing room.

"One lousy poster in a barber shop window isn't advertising," he grumbled. I didn't know what the problem was until we went on stage. Only about 600 of the 2,800 seats had warm, breathing bodies in them. Someone had dropped the ball on promoting the gig. Pee-Wee blamed the folks at Carnegie Hall. I don't know about that, but there's one thing I know for sure: I'd love to have one of those posters. I've looked and looked, and I can't find one. If you have a relative who owned a barber shop in New York City, go take a look in his attic. You never know.

One of the tour stops was in Canada. As we were driving along, Red announced, "Fifteen minutes to the border." Suddenly, all around me, the guys started opening their shirts and taping little packages to their bodies. *What the hell is this all about?* I thought. When we got to the border the customs officer didn't bother to inspect the bus. He stepped on board, looked at us with a smile, and said, "Have a good show," and left. There was a palpable feeling of relief around me.

When the tour ended in Omaha on October 11th, we were all scheduled to fly home from there. Harry and the band had a booking on *The Tonight Show*, which was still in New York, and they had to fly out on the 12th. Red was to take me to the Omaha airport for a different flight to New York.

Showbiz tradition has it that you always have a wrap party when a show, movie, whatever, wraps up. One of the guys decided to throw the party in his hotel room. I have to say this once again, I was very naïve. I smoked cigarettes in those days and had an occasional cocktail, but that's as far as it went. I was sitting in a chair when one of the guys came up with a pipe in his hand and told me to try it. I'd been around the business for a while and even worked in the Village where you could get anything, but I had never indulged in anything but alcohol. I figured, how bad could it be? I took one hit, and the next thing I knew it was like waves coming at me. My eyes closed and my head nodded forward. Sometime later, I don't know how long, the piano player lifted my chin with his hand, looked me in the eyes, and announced, "He's one of us!" I guess I wasn't "the kid" after that. The next day Red drove me to the airport to catch my flight back to New York. That was some seriously heavy-duty hashish they'd given me, and I was still hammered. I smiled all through the long drive to the airport, all through the flight, and I was still feeling the effects the next day.

There was one final odd moment on the tour. In those days you would see these little statues of jockeys in people's yards. The jockey would have a ring in his hand, supposedly where you would tie up your horse. No one rode horses, of course, but they had the statues anyway. I suppose this wasn't any stranger than putting plastic pink flamingoes in your yard. People are odd. Anyway, Red wanted one of those jockey statues to take home with him, and he got a lead on a local place in Omaha that sold them. On the way to dropping me off at the airport, off we went, high up on a hill on a road that twisted back and forth until we came to a huge garden filled with outdoor knick-knacks. Red found a jockey that met his standards for that kind of thing, but when he got back to the bus there was a crowd standing by.

The bus had a big sign that read Harry James Orchestra over the windshield and the crowd was clamoring for Harry. "Where's Harry James?" they were shouting.

Red was quick to respond. "I left him back in the garden." Off we went to the airport, with me still smiling.

Back in New York things returned to normal—that is, I was unemployed again. I went out and scrounged up the usual assortment of odd jobs until the next showbiz engagement arrived. Fortunately, I didn't have to wait long. One of early television's most recognizable performers, Garry Moore, got a new show in the fall of 1966 and I was cast in it. Garry had been very successful in radio and made a seamless transition to television. With his trademark crew cut and bowtie, he was all over the small screen, from game shows to variety shows, usually accompanied by his friend and second banana, Durward Kirby. His show would be the old variety format, but with new faces. I would be appearing with Jackie Vernon, Lily Tomlin, Pete Barbutti, and Chuck McCann. The show had a lot of promise, but the scripts weren't the best. I had the feeling that the writers were putting more time into polishing their resumes than the material, looking for their next gig. It didn't come as a shock when the show was cancelled midseason, but it was a disappointment.

It was during the last couple of episodes of the Moore show that I learned I wouldn't have to go back into the labor market when it was over. I'd been booked for a great job working with Mel Tormé and Woody Herman and The New Thundering Herd orchestra. We were set to perform at the famous Basin Street East in Manhattan, and we packed the house every night. Working with Mel was great and we had a lot of laughs. After the shows Mel, his recent bride Jan Scott, a British actress who was cute as a button, and I would go out for a late dinner and it was always a whole lot of fun. It was during this engagement that I met another show business legend who was to become a lifelong friend.

Mel was out working the room one night and I stood backstage waiting for my cue. I went out, did my first bit, and I heard a laugh that was recognizable to millions of television viewers. It was kind of a laugh-cackle. *Geez*, I thought, *Steve Allen is in the room*. I soon found out that Mel Tormé and Steve Allen were good buddies. They'd grown up together in Chicago and remained close through their professional careers. After my set that night the phone in my dressing room rang. It was Mel telling me to come up to his dressing room because someone wanted to meet me. It was Steve Allen. He told me how much he enjoyed my act and said that when he got another show I was going to be on it. He pulled out a little notebook and wrote himself a note about it. Steve was famous for writing his thoughts down as he went through the day and later working them into material. Steve and his wife, Jayne Meadows, became great friends of mine. He was incredibly talented and thoroughly unique. It was a heartbreak when he left us.

Mel Tormé was an all-around good guy and I really enjoyed working with him. Shortly after the Basin Street East gig he invited me to join him at the Blue Room at the Tropicana Hotel in Las Vegas—a beautiful place—with Si Zentner and His Orchestra. This was my first trip west and I ended up seeing a little more of it than I expected. While we were in Las Vegas, Steve Allen got a new show and, true to his word, he booked me on it. That was great, except Steve's show was in Los Angeles. If you don't have a map handy, that's a three-hundred-mile commute.

So, the epic round trip began. After performing with Mel at the Tropicana, I'd hop a plane for LA and be on Steve's set the next morning for rehearsal. When that wrapped I headed back to the airport to catch a plane to Las Vegas and be back performing with Mel at the Blue Room that night. This was all terrific and I would never change it, but I have to admit it was about as tiring as it could get. I actually developed the ability to sleep on an airplane. This led to a literal rude awakening. I had fallen asleep on the way to LA when I was awakened by the announcement, "We will be landing at Ontario in a minute." For a horrific moment I thought I had accidentally boarded a flight to Canada and missed the rehearsal. Then, to my relief, I learned that there was an airport in Ontario, California, and that we were just doing a stop on the way to LAX.

I was staying at the Tropicana Hotel during that engagement, but Mel and his wife were staying at a nearby condo. One night before the show, I had just finished putting on my tuxedo when there was a knock at the door. I opened it to find Mel holding the leash of a beautiful German Shepherd sitting patiently at his feet.

"Well, what do you think?" I acknowledged that it was a good-looking dog. "Want to know how I got him?" he asked. "I'll tell you how I got him. Everyday I'd go out on the balcony of the condo where Jan and I are staying and I'd look down into the yards at the back of the houses below, and in this one yard I noticed a dog tied up with no water to drink in sight. After noticing this for a few days I stopped by the house and knocked on the door, and when the guy answered, I told him that if I saw the dog with no water again I'd take him. Here he is."

For the next seven years that dog—Mel named him Thor—rode shotgun in Mel's Rolls Royce around Beverly Hills. That was Mel. Multi-talented guy, good friend, and a humane dognapper.

# Chapter Six

## *Small Screen, Big Audience*

The world moves incredibly fast these days. It was only a little over one hundred years ago that man learned to fly, and now we're sending satellites far out into our solar system. If you don't think that's fast, consider how many thousands of years it took man to come up with indoor plumbing. Judging by cave paintings, we've had the desire to perform or create art since we first popped up on this planet. I imagine eons ago there were cavemen standing on boulders telling jokes hoping to impress a few of the cave booking agents and, perhaps, a cave lady or two. The basic premise remains, but technology has left its stamp on the process.

I was born in the days of radio just as television broadcasting was becoming a reality. World War II slowed it down a bit, but I hadn't become a teenager yet when the glowing tubes started appearing in electronics store windows and the living rooms of a few privileged neighbors. The first screens were small—smaller than an iPad—but they got bigger and so did the business. TV opened up a world that was larger than many a kid my age ever imagined. The cave comics were still around, probably telling some of the same jokes, but now the boulder sat in your living room.

I got my first look at television long before I ever dreamed of performing on it, or anywhere, for that matter. We were living in Bohemia on Long Island. Bohemia was a small town at the time and most of the citizens knew one another. There were two streetlights and a general store that sold everything from canned goods to tennis shoes. A nice man named Mr. Chevanka owned the general store; he let his customers, including my mom, charge their purchases until payday. This was long before credit cards. People promised to pay and they did. I doubt that Mr. Chevanka ever got burned for his kindness and trust. It was that kind of place. It wasn't exactly the Mayberry of *The Andy Griffith Show*, but if it had been I would've been the red-haired Opie.

It was in 1948 that my friend Harry Paul had the good fortune of having his parents invest in one of the new gadgets. I remember it well. We trekked over to Harry's house to see the new Tele-King model with the twelve-inch screen. We turned it on and waited for the tubes to warm up, and slowly a flickering picture came into view, casting a weird blue light over everything. Pure magic. The greatest communication device ever known to man was sitting in Harry's living room.

His mother took full advantage of the new cultural opportunity: she watched wrestling. She had a favorite wrestler to cheer for, a guy named Gene Stanlee. He was a beefy, blond Adonis who tore up the ring like a wild man. Just the thing to perk up an evening in a sleepy little town. Mr. and Mrs. Paul were good people and would occasionally invite us kids over to catch some of the afterschool shows, like the *Time for Beany* puppet show, the cowboy exploits of the heroic *Hopalong Cassidy*, and Buster Crabbe as *Flash Gordon*. It didn't get much better than that for a kid, especially during those Long Island winters when sitting in that comfortable blue light beat the heck out of a face full of blowing snow.

Two of our other friends in the neighborhood, the twin Coster brothers, had the TV to end all TVs. It had a full twenty-two-inch screen. The Coster family had a beautiful home across the street from their family business, a wax factory. There was money in wax, I guess. The family lived well. (On weekends when the factory was closed, the Coster twins, Tom, and I would hop on the electric forklifts and scoot around the otherwise quiet factory for hours, until the day I lost control of one of them and crashed into one of the large metal factory doors. I couldn't fix the damage, so there was nothing for me to do except turn myself in and plead guilty. When I confessed to Mr. Coster, I was sentenced to a two-week ban from their family swimming pool, which to a kid during a Long Island summer is like two hundred years. At least I wasn't banned from their television.)

After Dad died and we moved in with our Aunt Annie and Uncle Joe in Elmhurst, Queens, we were able to watch their TV. This was the era of Jackie Gleason and Sid Caesar, and a budding juvenile comic couldn't have had a much better teacher than that glowing box in the living room. When Mom saved enough money to rent the apartment on McNish Street, we were TV-less again for about a year, but then Tom, Christine, and I heard about a big TV sale going on at the World's Fair Grounds in Forest Hills, New York. If we would have invested as much effort in our studies as we did coaxing Mother to go to the sale, we each would have a PhD today. Mom gave in.

After a trip on "the El"—the elevated train—to Forest Hills, the Biener family went into conference under a large sales tent in a parking lot and selected a seventeen-inch Admiral table model to become the new entertainment center for the household. We impatiently waited for it to be delivered, but it was worth the wait. Suddenly the *Arthur Godfrey and His Friends* show, with the Chordettes and Julius La Rosa,

Sky King, the Lone Ranger, and a host of other celebrities were making regular appearances in our living room.

After my sister Min married Stan, they bought a two-story house in Rockville Centre, Long Island, at Morris and Dartmouth streets. It was actually two homes in one building, and Mom, Christine, Tom, and I moved into the second floor, two-bedroom, one-bath unit. Tom and I had our own room, complete with separate beds. The trusty seventeen-inch Admiral became a portable when Tom and I lugged it up the stairs.

Without a doubt, that seventeen-inch Admiral had a major impact on my comedic development. I don't think it was just the opportunity to see and hear new voices to mimic. Every time that set lit up, it was a subtle reminder that there were people in the world who got to entertain other people for a living. I didn't sit there and ponder that all day, of course, but the fact remained that there were people on TV who brought happiness into people's lives. If they could do it, maybe anyone could do it. Exactly how that happened remained to be seen, but the point was that it was possible.

It was impossible to be around in that period without recognizing the major impact the new medium was having on society. The entire country virtually stopped on Monday nights for a half hour while it watched *I Love Lucy* on CBS. People were introduced to cultural aspects that they would never else have seen. A Catholic priest by the name of Bishop Fulton J. Sheen had a prime-time evening show on which he gave advice and encouragement to people of all faiths. On another channel at the same time, "Uncle Miltie," Milton Berle, was recycling his old vaudeville act, frequently in a woman's dress, to the delight of people across the country. He was so popular that in 1951 NBC gave him a thirty-year contract at $200,000 a year, a lot of money in those days. (Or today.) Lawrence Welk, a bandleader from South Dakota with a strange accent, came up with the concept of "champagne" dance music and blew bubbles and accordion solos into his studio audience for a couple of decades. You could see the New York Philharmonic Orchestra performing on one channel and, for a change of pace, go a couple of numbers up the dial to see the bad-guy wrestler smashing the good-guy wrestler's head into the turnbuckle. There was definitely something for everyone.

With that in mind, I figured there certainly should be a place for me.

A good chunk of my career—the majority of it, I guess—has been on television. Despite the fact that I worked on my character voices and watched a lot of TV when I was young, I never really consciously put the two together or created a plan to crack into the business. It just kind of happened, like that night at the Vanguard. I was just up there doing my act when Jack Babb walked in and brought TV to me.

My first near-brush with TV fame happened while I was a student at Southside High School in Rockville Centre. My friend Dean's dad, Joe Calcagno, had an in at another popular TV show of the time called *Name That Tune*. The concept for *Name That Tune* was pretty simple. Two contestants faced off against one another in the studio in front of the audience and the orchestra began to play a song. When the contestants recognized the song they rang a bell; the first bell ringer got a chance to name the tune. Anyone with knowledge of popular music and a perky personality had a shot. The personality thing mattered—a lot. If you've spent any time at all watching game shows, you will have noticed that the contestants jump, scream, clap, and do everything but wet themselves when they compete. The producers like energy, they like smiles, they want to see people having fun. Just knowing the answers isn't all that entertaining. Joe Calcagno managed to get me an audition in New York City where the producers could evaluate my energy and all-around entertainment quotient. Fine with me.

The audition didn't take place on the actual *Name That Tune* set, probably because the real set was in use for the show. Instead, they had a mock set in another area that they used for auditions. It looked pretty close to the real thing. The host for the actual show was the popular Bill Cullen, who had a long career in the game show business. Since Cullen was also tied up with the real show, we had a stand-in announcer. He was not at all close to the real thing. He looked like he lived on whiskey. My guess was that his next career move would be announcing departures at the Greyhound station. Anyway . . . a gig is a gig.

We got to the studio and I received the usual instructions about how the whole thing was going to work. They told me where to stand, the announcer introduced me, and I walked out to play the game. It started with the usual questions: what's your name, where are you from, how old are you, etc. Pretty hard to mess that up—all I had to do was answer energetically. Then we got around to the business at hand: they started to play the tunes. I had this knocked. I knew every song they threw at us and I was unbeatable. That's where the trouble started. It seems they felt it wasn't very interesting if the contestants immediately named the tunes. They wanted some drama. They wanted to see a little anxiety on the faces of the contestants as they struggled to come up with the right title. They wanted the audience at home to be yelling the answers at their TV sets to encourage us.

They suggested that I stumble over my answers and make an occasional mistake. The example they gave me was, instead of "Row, Row, Row Your Boat" I should answer, "Row, Row, Row Your Raft," or "Row, Row, Row Your Canoe." Seriously. Pretending to bungle something complicated was one thing, but "Row, Row, Row Your Canoe"? That wasn't going to happen. I wasn't about to return to school with my friends thinking that I was a complete moron. I said I wouldn't do it and that was the name of *that* tune. Some other lucky person got to look like an idiot on TV.

Speaking of not looking your best on TV, or anywhere else for that matter, it's kind of a drag when people continually mispronounce your name. As I mentioned earlier, the family name was originally Buehner and my grandparents emigrated from Biene, Germany. Through either haste, bad penmanship, or a strange sense of humor, the immigration folks at Ellis Island combined this into a new family name of Biener, pronounced *B*-ner. Unfortunately, teachers and classmates could never quite master that pronunciation and I always ended up being called Beaner or Beans.

This trend continued when I started doing talent shows. The hosts would invariably mess up my name by calling me Johnny Beaner, Johnny Bi-enner, or something even worse. By the time I started seriously considering entering show business, it was evident that I was either going to spend half my career correcting people or I had to come up with a simpler spelling. I chose option two, and in 1963 at the courthouse in Mineola, New York, John Biener was erased from the phone book and John Byner appeared for good. The rest of the family kept the old spelling; the girls until they got married and Tom

("Why should I change my name just because my brother is in show biz?") forever.

And now, back to the story . . .

Thanks to the continued support of Joe Calcagno and the fortunate intervention of Jack Babb, I wasn't totally banished from the small screen. Merv Griffin's *Talent Scouts* got me rolling and Ed Sullivan made me a household name, but it was a chance meeting when I was working with Mel Tormé at Basin Street East that led not only to some exciting TV work, but a friendship that lasted a lifetime. I had no idea how much that first appreciative, cackling laugh from Steve Allen would mean to my professional and personal future.

Like Ed Sullivan, it's hard today to imagine the impact that Steve Allen had on the young television industry, particularly television comedy. He was the son of vaudevillians, so maybe his talent was hereditary, but wherever it came from he had a ton of it. He was a performer, writer, composer, and something of a philosopher. Aside from his overall likability, his greatest gift may have been an incredible ability to ad-lib hilarious lines. Early in his career, when he had a radio show, he would frequently take a microphone into his studio audience and turn conversations with average people into comedy gold. Later, on television, he took his microphone and cameras onto the streets of Hollywood with equal success, a technique that has been copied by others for decades. His spontaneous humor and thunderous laugh were his trademarks.

Not only was Steve a major talent, but he was a master of recognizing and nurturing other people's talent. On his Sunday night *The Steve Allen Show* he had a comedic supporting cast that was next to none. Tom Poston, Louis Nye, Bill Dana, Don Knotts, Pat Harrington Jr., and Dayton Allen all played characters on the show on their way to stardom as

Steve generously set them up playing the straight man, with an occasional ad-lib of his own thrown in. As an adolescent I watched all of this on our trusty seventeen-inch Admiral. I can't really express what it felt like years later to have Steve Allen tell me he wanted me on his next show. That was beyond a big deal.

As I mentioned, my first show with Steve involved a daily six-hundred-mile round-trip commute so that I could work with Mel Tormé at the Tropicana Hotel in Las Vegas at night while rehearsing Steve's show in Hollywood during the day. Fortunately, at least from the standpoint of me getting some sleep, Mel's show only had a few more weeks to run in Las Vegas, so when it closed I was able to move to Los Angeles and work normal-people hours. Again, Steve had surrounded himself on the show with top-notch talent. He was never afraid that someone might be "too funny" and upstage him. To the contrary, Steve knew it was all about the show. The most important thing was to entertain the audience and make them laugh. If someone else made them laugh harder than he did once in a while, so be it. For a performer, particularly one like me who was fairly new to the business, that kind of support was invaluable.

The show was done at CBS Television City in the Fairfax District of Los Angeles. Unlike the studios in New York, which were generally converted theaters or radio studios, Television City was purposely built for the new medium. There was ample space to put up sets, cameras, and mic booms, and most importantly, accommodate a large studio audience. The audience was crucial to a show like Steve's. A performer wants to hear the response of real people. Comedians in particular want to hear those laughs. It's just not the same to perform without an audience with the idea that someone will put a laugh track on the show later. The difference is like night and day. Funny people want to hear a response. On this particular show there was an abundance of funny people. I joined Ron Carey, Ruth Buzzi, Jayne Meadows, and Louis Nye. With a cast like that Steve figured he could do just about anything. He was right.

Humans are funny creatures. When they get together in audiences—or juries—you never know what you're going to get. I've seen talented people get up on stage and absolutely kill one night, and then perform to near silence the next night in the same room with a different audience. I've had it happen to me. Why? They can't all have had a bad day. Is it the phase of the moon? Barometric pressure? I've never figured it out, but it happens. It actually happened on the first show we did in that series, and it was a good example of how well Steve understood audiences. Ron Carey was on stage doing a bit, but the audience wasn't quite with him. They were laughing, but the material and Ron were a lot better than the response he was getting. Steve stepped out on stage and to everyone's surprise, especially mine, announced that we were going to have a quick meeting and then we would be back. He led us to a conference room down the hall and told us that wherever we were when someone else was performing, we were to laugh. Loudly. If we were in the wings for a quick costume change and we heard a punchline, we laughed. The wardrobe lady laughed. The stagehands laughed. Most importantly, Steve laughed with that unique cackle that was irresistibly funny in itself. It worked. The audience warmed up, but honestly, I got the biggest kick of all watching Steve belt out that big laugh of his over his shoulder toward the stage while he was working on something else. That's showbiz.

I was a huge fan of Steve Allen and I'm honored to say

he was a huge fan of mine. He would see things in my act, cackle that big laugh, and then repeat those bits for years. On many occasions I saw him guesting on a talk show and quoting something he'd heard me do in my act. He wasn't stealing the joke, mind you—he always gave me the credit. It's an enormous honor when this kind of attention comes from someone who is an acknowledged genius in your field. It's a special feeling that's hard to describe.

Years later, Steve did a late-night talk show from the Palace Theater on Hollywood and Vine. Occasionally a guest would have to drop out at the last minute for one reason or another and Steve would call me to step in as a replacement. He knew I always had a ton of material and that I could ad-lib with him as well. One night I was sitting in his green room watching the show when the person who went on before me, an author, tripped going up onto the small riser where Steve's desk and the guest chairs were. No big deal, but it gave me an idea. When it was my turn and Steve announced me, I stepped up onto the riser, pretended to trip, and crashed into everything in sight. Steve broke into absolute hysterical laughter that went on and on. When he got control of himself, he told me on the air that I made him feel like he was back in high school. I loved making Steve *really* laugh. For me there was no higher praise.

I became great friends with Steve and his wonderful wife, Jayne Meadows. The two of them were inseparable and were an all-around great Hollywood couple. Steve and Jayne were always up for contributing to a worthy cause, and when they participated in fundraisers they would frequently give me a call to join them. Steve's creative mind never stopped, and he constantly filled his ever-present notebook, and later voice recorder, with his ideas. He'd often get an idea that he thought would work well in my act and send it to me to consider. In a business where people tend to only think of themselves, Steve was a guy who was happy to help everyone. After we moved out of Los Angeles Steve and Jayne would invite my wife Annie and me to stay with them when I came back into town for a job. They were both terrific, talented, and creative people. I, like many, many people who knew Steve, treasure the time I spent with him and will always miss him.

It wasn't too long after the Steve Allen series that I got my first opportunity to host a series of my own. It's a big jump from being a piece of the show to being the glue that holds all the pieces together. By this time I had done enough television to be very comfortable and confident, but still, this was a big step up.

The series was produced by Robert E. Petersen Productions. Robert Petersen was a heavy hitter in the magazine world. His company published *Car Craft*, *Rod and Custom*, *Sports Car Graphic*, and *Motor Trend* magazines, among several other automotive titles. He was also a firearms enthusiast and headed some publications in that area, such as *Guns and Ammo*. When you entered his office you were confronted by a world-class taxidermy project, an enormous, stuffed white bear. The thing looked like it was ten or eleven feet tall. Huge. The story was that he had shot it from a helicopter. I don't know if that's true, but the size of the thing was astounding. In 1994 he established the Petersen Automotive Museum in Los Angeles, which is a monument to his love for cars.

Back in the '60s he decided to branch out into the television business. He probably realized that a lot of the young people who read his car magazines were also caught up in the music revolution going on at the time. His company came up with a music-oriented show called *The Action Faction*. It was a pretty good idea. A host—me—would travel around the country to where singers and bands lived and film them performing in their cities. Each episode would be shot at some interesting area in their town, and to add to the excitement we brought along a cast of very talented young ladies who performed as the "Action Faction Dancers." I thought the whole thing was great and was happy to be doing it, except for one thing. I hated the title. "The Action Faction" just seemed to get stuck in my mouth. I mentioned this to the producer, Robert Dellinger, one day and he asked me if I had a better idea.

"I don't know," I said, "just something else."

"I like that," he said, "we'll call it *Something Else.*" *Something Else* seemed to work for the show, and the dance troupe remained the Action Faction Dancers, which also seemed pretty good. Everyone was happy.

In addition to Robert Petersen and Robert Dellinger, we had a very solid production team. The dancers were choreographed by Bob Banas and Anita Mann, and the series was directed by Donn Cambern, who was hot off the classic film *Easy Rider*, which he edited, and who would go on to a long, successful career as editor of many of the top feature films of the era, such as *The Cannonball Run* and *Romancing the Stone*.

The musical acts were also the cream of the crop for that period. Linda Ronstadt sang on the beach in San Diego. O. C. Smith performed on a dock in Newport Beach, California. We shot Three Dog Night in Sausalito and Pete Fountain in New Orleans. We had Merrilee Rush, Jimmy Webb, Johnny Mathis, Lou Rawls, The Guess Who, Richie Havens, Taj Mahal, Tony Joe White, The Beach Boys, Lou Christie, Credence Clearwater

Revival, The Grass Roots, The Turtles, Ricky Nelson, Iron Butterfly, The Carpenters, Roy Clark, Gary Puckett and the Union Gap, Dion, Lulu . . . whew! I look at those names today and I'm still impressed. We went on the air in the spring of 1970 and it would be hard to name another show that had more singing, dancing, comedy, and great locations than we did. Looking back now, the whole thing was like a cultural time capsule of the period.

As the host I handled the comedy end of things and the writers came up with plenty of clever ideas to make my job interesting. We were shooting in San Diego where there was a large, old, four-masted ship docked as a tourist attraction. The writers thought it would be a funny bit to have me on the ship in a pirate outfit, complete with a large three-pointed hat on my head and stuffed parrot on my shoulder. The jacket had brass buttons with a wide belt, and the boots came up over my thighs and had kneecaps. To top off the whole look, I held a dagger in my teeth. It looked great with me bundled up like that on the deck of that beautiful ship, but there was a little more to the bit.

The script called for me to climb the rigging to the crow's nest at the top of the center mast while the girls danced on deck to "pirate music." I love the ocean and I love ships, but climbing rope rigging while bound up in a costume, chewing on a knife, was a pretty far cry from what I had done in the navy. It looked like a long way up to the crow's nest from the deck. They rolled the camera and off I went, step by step on the shaky ropes until I finally got to the top of the mast. From there, it looked like a long way down. I hung on for dear life until I heard the magic word, "Cut!" I slowly worked my way down the rigging to safety where I heard, "Okay, let's do one more take." Oh, great. So the camera rolled, the music started playing, the girls started dancing, I stuck the dagger in my teeth, and off I went on my way to the crow's nest again. I huffed and puffed about three quarters of the way up the rigging when I apparently opened my mouth to breathe. Out slipped the dagger and I watched it fall a looong way to the deck. Fortunately, the dagger landed harmlessly. I slowly climbed down from the rigging to the deck and finally exhaled. To my relief, everyone figured we had enough footage of me in the rigging.

Every show opened with a dance number featuring the girls and me in some particularly visual area of the city we were visiting. In Los Angeles the writers selected the rooftop of a multi-story building downtown and decided it would look great to fly me down in a helicopter. I'd never been on a helicopter before, but the whole bit sounded interesting. However, when the helicopter arrived it was one of those very little ones that looks like a soap bubble with a tail. They'd rigged a fake control stick into the cockpit so it looked like I was actually piloting the thing, and up we went. So far, so good.

It was coming back down that became the white-knuckle experience. Through the clear Plexiglas floor of the chopper the buildings and steeples of the downtown area looked like shark's teeth, and I was fully aware that the rotor was spinning away around us as we descended. To make it worse, as we got close to the buildings the turbulence from the rotor blades started bouncing the chopper all over the place. I suppose that if you do this all the time you get used to it, but for a first flight it wasn't making me very happy. We bounced around a few hundred feet over the rooftop as the girls danced below us, waiting for our cue to land. Finally it came. And then . . . they wanted take two. And three. And finally, take eight. The series was sponsored by the National Dairy Council and there was a whole lot of milk-drinking on the set. By the time we finished that scene I felt like I'd been churned into butter.

I hosted twenty-two episodes of *Something Else* that year. The problem was, they shot twenty-four episodes. The show was great and we were all having a ball. As the season was drawing to a close, I decided I wanted to have a wrap party at my house. It wasn't anything wild, just the cast and crew hanging out having fun. Somewhere along the line someone lit a joint and that turned into a story that got spun completely out of control. The odor was reported to the production company and alarm bells started ringing. Who knows what the story was by the time it circulated to the top, but it's safe to say it had to be a whole lot more embellishment than the truth. Maybe it was just that it was against the squeaky-clean image of the sponsor, the National Dairy Council, and the production company wanted to avoid any potential problems with them.

Whatever the case, Robert Dellinger got a hold of me and told me my hosting duties had come to an end. He hired Johnny Hartford to host the last two episodes. I found out later that Hartford had been his first pick, so maybe it just took him twenty-two episodes to find a way to get rid of me. It was a bitter pill to swallow, since I hadn't done anything more than own the home where the party was, but that didn't seem to matter to anyone but me. Dellinger ended up with his own set of issues. After some problems in his life he concocted a scheme to extort $200,000 each from four airlines. The escapade ended in a gunfight with the FBI and a trip to federal prison.

The National Dairy Council probably wouldn't have liked that much, either.

# Chapter Seven

## *"Here's Johnny(s)"*

For thirty years late-night television was dominated by one program: *The Tonight Show Starring Johnny Carson*. No one knew he was on his way to being a late-night legend when he became the host of the show in 1962, but from the first night he stepped in front of that multicolored curtain—NBC's way of showing off their relatively new color studios—it was pretty clear that the clean-cut, boyish-looking Nebraskan, a former magician and game show host, had the one quality that was exactly what the network was looking for: he appealed to everyone. In terms of prestige, appearing on *The Tonight Show* was the late-night equivalent of appearing on *The Ed Sullivan Show*. It was a particularly good boost for comedians, since the show heavily favored humor. The idea was to give the audience something funny to ease them off to sleep, sort of the antidote for the news. With that in mind I was looking forward to my audition for the show. Unfortunately, it didn't go anywhere near as well as I hoped. In fact, it didn't go at all.

It's hard to imagine it now, but until the 1970s America pretty much rolled up the television sidewalks at 1:00 a.m. People watched the late news, weather, and sports and went to bed. Local TV stations might run a thirty-year-old movie for the sake of the diehard night owls, but by 1:00 a.m. they usually signed off the air with a picture of the American flag accompanied by the national anthem, and then the glowing tube faded to black for five or six hours.

It was my friend, Steve Allen, in one of his many moments of genius, who recognized that there was a large audience for fresh entertainment between the news and sign-off. He cooked up a forty-minute experiment on WNBT-TV in New York in 1954 that pushed all of America's buttons. It was the perfect combination of comedy and music that sent the country to bed with a smile on its face. He called it *The Tonight Show* and it was quickly picked up on the NBC network, which expanded it to 105 minutes. Late-night television was born. Steve left the show in 1957 to focus on a prime-time career, and Jack Paar took over as host for five years. Then came Johnny Carson, and he and *The Tonight Show* became legendary.

As Johnny climbed to the top of the television ladder, I was still quite a few rungs below. Like pretty much everyone else who ever started in the business, my first step was to get out into the world and show people what I could do. About this time a Broadway producer named Budd Friedman decided to open a coffee house in Manhattan that catered to the theatrical crowd. He named it The Improvisation, but that club and all the others that eventually followed became known simply as The Improv. At first The Improv stage hosted a pretty impressive roster of Broadway luminaries, particularly from the world of music. However, it wasn't long before comedians became the dominant entertainment force and a whole new business model was formed: the comedy club. Budd eventually created his own comedy empire and even hosted the popular *An Evening at the Improv* television series that ran for many years and was produced by the co-writer of this book, Doug Wellman.

For a young comic The Improv was the perfect showcase venue. If a television show talent coordinator was looking for fresh new comics, The Improv was full of them, trying out new material and mingling with their fellow hopefuls. One of them was me.

One night after my set at The Improv I met a guy named John Carsey and we became instant friends. That happens sometimes—people just click. John liked my routines and we had a lot of laughs. After a while John suggested that I go down to his office with him and do my act for his boss. John was a writer for *The Tonight Show*. He didn't have to ask me twice; this was clearly a golden opportunity.

*The Tonight Show* was still in New York in those days, as it was for most of the first decade of Johnny Carson's reign. John set up an audition for the following week, and I went through the standard ritual of choosing my bits and rehearsing them before putting on my suit and driving into the city for my appointment at Rockefeller Center, commonly known as 30 Rock. Once inside the Kingdom of NBC I took an elevator to the appointed floor, where John was waiting for me. We had a quick chat and then John took me to *The Tonight Show* offices and introduced me to the receptionist. She pointed toward the door. I knocked, and I was invited in. My big shot had come.

After all these years I don't actually remember who I was auditioning for. I remember thinking at the time that the three guys in the small room I had entered were writers. Could they have been producers or talent coordinators? Maybe. All I know for sure is that there were three of them stuffed into a small office with a desk.

We probably made a bit of small talk—I don't really recall—but if there was any it wasn't much. They wanted to get down to business, which was just fine with me. The guy sitting in the swivel chair behind the desk seemed to be in charge, and he finally looked at me and said, "Let's see what you've got." I started to go into the setup for my first bit and managed to get out a half-dozen words before I heard Swivel Chair Guy say, "Who wants coffee?" I stopped and looked at the two other straight-faced guys and waited for their answer. "No, don't stop," Swivel Chair Guy said. "Just go on." I picked up where I'd left off, said a few words and then heard, "So, who wants coffee?" I stopped again, took a last look at my rude hosts, turned, and walked out the door.

I wasn't going to put up with that. It's hard to be a performer. When you perform in a room of people, no matter how many or how few there are, everything becomes personal. You are your act. Criticism of your performance is personal criticism. There's no way around that. That kind of rudeness is a personal wound and it hurts. Those three guys were professionals and they should have known better. Or maybe Swivel Chair Guy was just a jerk and enjoyed tormenting people, like a kid who pulls the wings off of flies. I wasn't going to be his victim, *Tonight Show* or no *Tonight Show*. John Carsey was waiting outside for me, anxious to see how it had gone. I told him, and then thanked him for being a good friend and for trying. After that it was the long, bitter drive back to Long Island.

Fortunately, this story has a happy ending for everyone. John and I remained good friends and he introduced me to his then-fiancée, Marcy, who also became a good friend. We continued to pal around the island of Manhattan and always had a good time, and then we each got a break in our own ways. John and Marcy got married and John became the head writer of *The Tonight Show*. After a stint as a network executive, Marcy went on to found the Carsey-Werner Company with Tom Werner, which produced *The Cosby Show*, *A Different World*, *Roseanne*, *Grace Under Fire*, *3rd Rock from the Sun*, and *That '70s Show*. And me? Well, I was popping up all over TV and developing a following, so in 1967 I was invited to pop through the multi-colored curtain for the first of my thirty-seven appearances with Johnny on *The Tonight Show*.

It's my job to entertain the audience, of course, but I also get a kick out of entertaining my showbiz associates. They like a good laugh as much as the next guy, and over the years I've occasionally had special requests. For example, one day I got a call from my manager informing me that he'd received a request for me to appear on *The Tonight Show*. I thought that was a little unusual, since I had just guested on the show and they usually didn't rebook guests that frequently. My manager agreed with me but told me that they had booked Orson Welles on the show, and it was Welles who asked if I could be on the same episode. Welles was an entertainment giant (in many ways), so I was honored by the request and accepted the booking.

On show night he was on immediately ahead of me, so I sat and watched on the green room monitor as he and Johnny bantered in front of an appreciative audience. They got around to talking about being a guest on a talk show, and Welles said to Johnny, "You know what bugs me? When you introduce a comic and they feel compelled to do some shtick just as they come through the curtain instead of waiting to get to their mark or the desk." That was all I needed to hear.

In a few minutes it was my turn to go on. I heard Johnny say, "And now here's comedian John Byner." The big multicolored curtain opened, and I launched myself onto the stage with a cartwheel. Then I walked over to Johnny, shook his hand, turned to Orson, and as I shook his hand said, "SEE!" He broke up. A really big man with a really big laugh. Music to my ears.

Sometimes the laugh was on me. On one *Tonight Show* appearance I had the honor of being booked with two of the most wonderful singer/dancer people in all of show business: Fred Astaire and Gene Kelly. I would later be cast with Astaire in the TV movie, *The Man in the Santa Claus Suit*, but this was the first time I'd met either him or Kelly. Not only was I on the same show, but I was seated between them on the panel. This was like being bookended by legends, and I was a bit awestruck. I looked at them and told them, with complete honesty, that I was really thrilled to be in their company. I added, "I know people who would pay a million dollars to be seated where I am."

They both turned to me and in unison, as though it had been rehearsed, said, "Where are they?!" Their timing was perfect. The audience, Johnny, and I all broke up.

When Johnny got the right mix of people on the panel, the results could be spectacular. *The Tonight Show* continued to raise the bar for TV comedy year after year. Combining Johnny with Dom DeLuise, Burt Reynolds, whipped cream, and eggs was an accidental work of genius. Booking comedy legends Bob Hope and Dean Martin with the perpetually hapless George Gobel was another. Some of those classic performances will live on YouTube forever. When you have quick minds together, particularly quick comedy minds, anything can happen.

I had a few of those special moments, but one sticks out in my memory. I was booked on *The Tonight Show* on the same night as Carl Reiner and Rose Marie. Carl had become a household name as an actor on *Your Show of Shows* with Sid Caesar in the 1950s, but his biggest successes were behind the scenes as a writer and director. In 1961 he created *The Dick*

*Van Dyke Show*, which became an instant television comedy classic and cleaned up on Emmy awards for the next six years. Rose Marie had been a child singer and film actress, originally billed as Baby Rose Marie, and then went into a successful career as a nightclub entertainer. She had a wonderful self-effacing sense of humor, frequently making jokes about her looks and age. She carried that trait over into her character, Sally Rogers, on *The Dick Van Dyke Show*. When it came to wisecracks, all of us were quick on the draw. We just needed something to set us off, and that was supplied by Johnny.

I had already gone out and done my bit, as had Carl, while Rose Marie waited backstage to join us on the couch. She didn't wait long. Johnny began her introduction with, "Our next guest has been in the business for a looong, looong, looong time," which was greeted by a groan from the audience.

Before he could continue, Rose Marie burst through the curtain, walked behind Johnny, and in a mock-threatening voice asked, "What did you say?"

Johnny began to stumble for an answer, but Carl piped up, "John Byner will tell you what he said!"

I jumped in immediately with, "He said when they built the first stage you were holding a hammer." The audience laugh was huge and Johnny almost fell out of his chair. With that, Rose Marie turned and marched offstage. After a beat, Carl and I looked at each other, stood, and followed her, leaving Johnny alone. The audience continued to roar. Suddenly alone with nothing to do, Johnny walked center stage and pulled off his jacket as Doc Severinsen and the band began to play "The Stripper." After shedding his shirt and tie he headed back to his desk, where Rose Marie joined him along with Carl and I, who had also removed our shirts. By this time the audience, the band, the crew, basically everyone in the studio, was in hysterics as Johnny shouted, "This is one of the wildest shows ever!"

One of my more unusual *Tonight Show* appearances was the night I was on the show without knowing I was going to be on the show. Surprise. It was a New Year's Eve and I wasn't performing anywhere, so I decided to have a relaxing evening at the ranch. The ranch was a beautiful two-acre site off of Ramirez Canyon in Malibu. Buying that property was something of a surprise in itself, since I wasn't looking for a house. I was killing time before meeting friends for dinner and stopped off at an open house for lack of anything better to do. When I saw the place, it was like a dream property I might've drawn as a school kid. There was a little stream, a garage with an upstairs studio, and lots and lots of beauty. So, in 1973 for a hot fifty-two grand, I became the owner of my very own little Malibu paradise. Emphasis on little, by the way. We're not talking about the Malibu mansions owned by Cher, Barbra Streisand, or their like. To the contrary, the house was like a large cabin and just oozed peace, tranquility, and charm. I'm not a mansion guy, so having my very own little nature park within commuting distance to Hollywood was like being in heaven.

The place became the ranch largely due to our family fondness for animals. The kids played a big role in that. If there was a stray anything within walking distance of the property, they brought it home. You know how it goes—you get one or two of this and one or two of that and the next thing you know you're Noah without the boat. Anyway, the kids had gone off to celebrate New Year's Eve at their friend's house on the beach, and I was looking forward to a little quiet time.

I was reclining on the floor in front of the fireplace with a glass of wine, watching Johnny, and feeling pretty good about everything. Johnny then announced, "I want to close the show with a guy I think is really funny." The next thing I saw was a montage of me doing bits from previous appearances on *The Tonight Show*. Johnny closed out his New Year's Eve show with him laughing at me. That was pretty special.

On the personal side Johnny and I had something in common. We're both shy. That's not entirely uncommon with performers, although it's certainly not the norm. We slip into a character or our act and are completely confident in front of an audience; however, we're sometimes a little uncomfortable just being ourselves. If you saw Johnny doing a bit like Art Fern, the Teatime Movie host, you would never believe there was a quiet guy underneath.

In our personal relationship Johnny would sometimes use humor to break the ice in otherwise mundane circumstances. I used to impersonate George Jessel, with his distinctive speech pattern, and Johnny loved it. When I would run into him backstage or in the makeup room at NBC he would frequently say hello to me using the Jessel voice and I would respond in the same way. We would both break up. It was a little bit like he always had to hide himself behind a joke.

Without engaging in some level of performance, Johnny could be a very quiet guy. We were both doing a fundraiser at the Santa Monica Civic Auditorium once for an organization called SHARE, which raises money for needy children. Jo Stafford was also on that show, and Frank Sinatra made a guest appearance, so it was a pretty big night. Johnny felt the need to escape all of the people and commotion at the afternoon rehearsal, so he invited me to join him in his dressing room motor home. Johnny made a pot of coffee and we sat down, and for the next twenty minutes we said practically nothing. Two guys who make their living performing in front of millions of people couldn't think of much to say to each other.

The traditional symbol of the theater is two masks, one frowning, one smiling, representing drama and comedy. That might be truer than some people expect. Some of us work very well behind the mask. It's real life that makes us uneasy.

Johnny was always a very gracious host to me when I did the show, and I only remember two instances where he made me uncomfortable. When you perform on a talk show like *The Tonight Show* there is usually a producer who discusses what you will be doing on the show and then writes some questions for the host to use to lead into your bits. We were going through this process one night. Johnny was setting me up with questions, I was giving the punchlines, and everyone was laughing. Everyone except Johnny. I began to feel like I was having a conversation with Mount Rushmore. Worse, he actually looked almost sullen. As I said earlier, there's no way a performer can take a response, or lack of response, as anything other than personal. You are what you are, and you're standing out there alone in front of God and everyone. I was getting a little concerned. I knew my material was good—the audience was roaring—and I couldn't understand why I wasn't hitting a home run with him.

I got my answer when we went to a commercial break. Johnny leaned across the desk and said, "I'm not laughing because this morning while at home in my office I dropped something on the floor and when I stood up I hit my tailbone on the corner of my desk. Right now I'm sitting on a rubber donut [to ease the pain]." I was relieved. "That's okay, Johnny, a smile will do."

Another night I got a very strange response from him when I was telling a story about the time I took my kids with me to the Hilton International Hotel in Las Vegas where I was performing with Glen Campbell. I explained to Johnny and the studio audience that it was my daughter Sandra's tenth birthday, so I took her, her younger sister Rosine, and brother Don with me so we could all have a birthday celebration together. About an hour outside of Las Vegas I was pulled over by a motorcycle officer for speeding. To make matters worse, in my haste to pack up the kids and hit the road, I'd left my driver's license at home. As I was standing behind my car trying to explain all of this to the officer, Sandra leaned out the car window and demanded, "Officer, if you arrest my father, who's going to take care of us?" The officer looked at Sandra, looked at me, and said, "Get out of here." The audience began to laugh, but Johnny was stone-faced as he sarcastically said loud enough for everyone to hear, "Oh, she said that, huh?" and we went to commercial. Ouch. I don't know what he was sitting on that night.

Aside from the fact that I generally enjoyed working with Johnny and a lot of interesting guests, appearing on *The Tonight Show* could also be a big career boost. The Ed Sullivan audience and the prime-time audience weren't necessarily the same people as the late-night audience. The late-night people also tended to be nightclub patrons, and in those days I was a real road warrior. I could show up for a booking at a club in Pittsburgh or Chicago or pretty much anywhere else and see the same marquee: "Direct from *The Tonight Show*, John Byner." Not only did the clubs sell out the seats, but I knew those seats would be filled with people who knew my work and were really looking forward to seeing me. It felt good.

Johnny had his faults. We all do. He had some ups and

downs in his personal life. We all do. However, one thing was certain: for that sixty to ninety minutes he was on the air five nights a week, he was the king of TV. No rivals.

John, age 7 and brother Tom, age 5.

Graduation from Boot Camp with mother and Tom.

John, and Ed Sullivan.

Ed Sullivan, John and John's family.

Harry James Playbill.

John and Johnny Carson.

Garry Moore, John, and Phil Silvers.

John and Don Rickles.

Sandra Byner and Elvis.

Bobbie Gentry poster.

John as Captain Hero, with Bea Arthur on "Maude".

Katherine Helmond, Robert Mandan, and John from "Soap."

John, Annette Funicello, and Frankie Avalon.

Carol Burnett and John.

The Great Smokey Roadblock poster.

"John Byner Comedy Hour."

Dinah Shore, John, and Sally Struthers.

John, Joseph Bologna, and Carol Kane from "Transylvania 6-5000."

John, Jim Nabors, Loni Anderson, Burt Reynolds, Ned Beatty,
and Bubba Smith from "Stroker Ace".

Burt Reynolds and John.

"Bizarre" T-shirt gag.

Golfing with Johnny Mathis.

"D.O.A."

# Chapter Eight

## *Six Hours of Stardom*

T he 1960s and 1970s were a great time for performers like me. In addition to a lot of great television sitcoms and dramas, it was a time when the comedy-variety show was popular. More often than not these shows were built around a popular recording artist, but also heavily featured sketch comedy using both a resident acting company and comedy and music guest stars. There was plenty of work in this field back then. If you had a *TV Guide* from that era you would see *The Sonny and Cher Show*, *The Dean Martin Show*, *The Mac Davis Show*, *The Smothers Brothers Show*, *The Andy Williams Show*, *The Flip Wilson Show*, and the groundbreaking *Laugh-In*. That's a whole lot of shows. A guy could make a living as a professional guest star.

One of the shows of that time, *The Glen Campbell Goodtime Hour*, was hosted by my good friend Glen Campbell. Glen was a great guy and an amazing musical talent. He grew up dirt poor, as they say, in Arkansas, the son of sharecroppers. As a child he picked cotton to help the family survive financially. An uncle gave him a cheap guitar and showed him a few chords, and after that Glen was on his own. A decade later he was on his way to a fantastic career as a singer-songwriter, making a couple of stops along the way to play in concert with The Beach Boys, and play as a studio musician with just about everyone.

It's not well known, but back then there was a small group of musicians in Hollywood who were in demand to play on all the top albums, frequently replacing the members of the actual band. Studio time was money, and they had to be able to sight-read music and perform flawlessly with not much of a rehearsal, so being an in-demand studio musician was really quite an honor. You had to be at the top of your game.

After a couple of big hits—"By the time I get to Phoenix" and "Wichita Lineman"—Glen was holding down a couple of slots on the Billboard Hot 100 chart. This was enough to get the attention of network TV programmers, and soon he was offered a summer replacement slot for *The Sonny and Cher Show*. The summer show drew an audience, so he was given his own series that ran from 1969 to 1972. The music on the show had a strong country feel to it and was popular with audiences; however, rumor had it that the wife of a top CBS executive was not a fan of country music and was anxious to see Glen nudged out of the way in favor of a more middle-of-the-road show. With that, Glen was canceled. CBS needed a summer replacement for Glen's show and my phone rang. *The John Byner Comedy Hour* was born.

We had a talented team of people behind the camera as well as in front of it. Rich Eustis, Jerry McPhie, Al Rogers, and Nick Sevano were the producers and the series was directed by Jack Regis. We had a repertory company of comic talent to play all the different characters each week, which included Patti Deutsch, Dennis Flannigan, Gary Mule Deer, Linda Sublette, R.G. Brown, and Bobby Grumbley Morris. The cast of a show is like a family. This family was crazy . . . in a really good way.

Writing an hour of funny material every week is a hard job. You have to be funny, and there can't be long pauses between the jokes. Writing is hard enough, but to write consistently funny is harder. I write my own club act, but that's a different story. I have a lot of time to work on bits, try them out, and then combine them into a longer performance. I could never create an hour of material every week while also rehearsing and shooting a show. Like everyone else in the world of television, I relied on a staff of writers to produce funny material and a lot of it. I was very fortunate to have a great writing staff for this, my first starring show.

Unlike those of us in front of the camera, most writers don't become household names. This was not the case on my show, since a few of them went on to receive public recognition. In fact, three of them, Craig T. Nelson, Barry Levinson, and Rudy De Luca, had been a team in the world of stand-up comedy, working primarily at The Comedy Store on the Sunset Strip, which Rudy had co-founded with comedian Sammy Shore, but in those days they were better known in Hollywood for their comedy writing chops. After my show they went off to great individual careers. Craig T. Nelson became an actor and eventually had a long, successful run as the star of the sitcom *Coach*. Barry Levinson became a motion picture writer-director and had tremendous success with movies like *Diner*, *Bugsy*, and *Rain Man*. Rudy De Luca has something of a zany streak and did a lot of work with Mel Brooks on films like *Spaceballs*, *History of the World, Part I*, and *Life Stinks*. Rudy and I teamed up again later on a film that he wrote and directed called *Transylvania 6-5000*, in which I played a character called Radu. Carol Kane played my wife Lupi, and the rest of the wonderful cast included Geena Davis, Jeff Goldblum, Ed Begley Jr., Joe Bologna, and Teresa Ganzel. Those guys have some serious comedy talent.

In those days, writers began with the misery of staring

at a blank piece of paper. They do the same thing today, only with a blank computer screen. The idea is to start with nothing and come up with something hilarious. That's a tall order. Writers look everywhere for a funny idea or something they can exaggerate into a funny idea. Sometimes they pull ideas from their own life, but often it's from the newspaper or just spending time studying people. Most people are too busy going about their own business to pay much attention to the people around them. That's too bad, because people can be very entertaining if you take the time to look at them. Simple little things like juggling a couple of grocery bags on the bus can be turned into comedy gold. If you want a couple of laughs take a look at your neighbors, and don't be surprised if they're looking at you.

The writing staff on my show took an interesting approach to coming up with material, one I hadn't heard of before. When I arrived for my first day at CBS Television City in Hollywood, the scene of many happy memories with Steve Allen, I was introduced to costume designer Ret Turner and his assistant. They were prepared with racks of costumes and I spent the day becoming a soldier, a Southern sheriff, an old prospector, a priest, a gangster, and on and on. They took pictures of me in each of those getups and sent them to the writers, and the guys used the pictures to think up crazy characters and situations. It was a pretty good idea, and certainly a lot better than staring at a blank piece of paper.

One of the sketches on the show was created around characters named The Bland Family. Their solution to every problem was cookies and ice cream. Then there was "Father O' Father," a parody of the priests in the movies that were played by Barry Fitzgerald, Bing Crosby, Spencer Tracy, and others. I modeled my character a bit on Fitzgerald, with an Irish accent and a kind of "tut-tut-tut" way of admonishing my congregation.

Father O' Father smoked a long, curved pipe, wore a long, black cassock, and counseled his troubled flock in his office at the church. Unfortunately, his troubled flock wasn't always all that confident in his advice. Whenever he was challenged, Father O' Father would announce that it was time to say goodbye for now, and would start to exit dramatically by walking through a series of pools of light like Jimmy Durante did at the end of the old *Jimmy Durante Show*, while muttering to himself about the importance of doing the right thing and all of the reasons people should pay more attention to him. By the time the good Father got to the third pool of light he had convinced them his advice was best and he'd shout, "I'm glad you see it my way," as he hurried back to the people he was counseling. After they left he would then celebrate by playing a record of Bing Crosby singing a chorus of the Irish lullaby "Too-Ra-Loo-Ra-Loo-Ral," which had become popular when Bing Crosby sang it while playing a priest in the 1944 film *Going My Way*. Father O' Father made it clear who his hero was, since he would hold a picture of Bing Crosby and talk to him as he danced: "Some people have to be told, but you know how to do it, Bing."

In one particular sketch Father O' Father admonished a couple by saying, "If you can't do something right, get out of the pool." A whistle had been inserted into his pipe. We did the sketch in rehearsal and it worked great, but in front of the audience, as I was making my exit through the pools of light, I realized I had the wrong pipe. No whistle. As I was about to deliver the line about the pool I saw the prop master holding the correct pipe frantically crawling my way while staying out of sight of the camera. He made it just in time; I reached out of the shot, switched pipes, and got it up to my face in time to whistle the punchline.

Another popular character was called Joe De Loser. He was your classic '50s high school dropout street corner punk, the last of his gang to still be hanging out in front of the candy store. Our hair and wardrobe people were a great help to me in creating that character. I had a greased back, D.A. hairdo— with a pompadour of course—black motorcycle boots, black pegged pants, and a white T-shirt with a pack of cigarettes rolled up in the right sleeve. Each sketch would begin with the opening bars of "Heartbreak Hotel" as Joe strutted onto the set of a big city street. Filled with himself, he sang (sort of) along with the song: "Dah, dah, dah, dah, dah, dah, dah, BOOM, and we're gonna rock TONIGHT!" As the king of his street corner he'd call out to any girl or guy from the neighborhood that got close, none of whom were actually seen on camera. "Hey, Judy, wanna go to the dance tonight?" Off-camera, one of the girls like Patty Deutsch would yell back, "Get a job!" He only had one response, no matter what was yelled at him, "RIIIGHT!" On one of the shows, done in pantomime, Joey got into a fight with an imaginary bad guy. He lost. "Oh, now try it with both hands!" he shouted defiantly as the winner walked away.

The one area where I was able to contribute to the writing of the show was in the monologue. I had a lot of material from my club act that could be restructured for the show by doing variations. I never limited myself to only doing impressions of famous people. As I walk through the world I see a lot of interesting creatures, and I'm able to put interesting voices with my physical actions. Take, for example, the tiny lizards that are common in various parts of the country, particularly the Southwest. I could see them through my window staring at me, looking like they were doing push-ups. What does a lizard think? How about a little song: "Although I wear a frown, I'm very hap-hap-happy!" Or an impression of the sandpiper bird on the beach that's been told not to get his feet wet. "Can't get my feet wet! Can't get my feet wet!" It's great fun to create characters of animals, and the audience always enjoyed it.

One of my opening monologues was an exception. I came into the office one Monday morning and walked into the writer's room where I ran into Barry Levinson, who asked me how my weekend had gone. "It's funny you should ask," I said, and then told him about someone I had met. When I finished the story Barry laughed and called the rest of the writers together to gather around, then he asked me to tell it again. When I finished, the verdict was unanimous: my weekend story was going to be that week's monologue.

The previous Saturday evening had started innocently enough. I'd stopped at The Comedy Store on Sunset Boulevard in West Hollywood to have a beer and catch an act or two. I'm really not all that big on socializing, but when I decide to go out what better place to go than one filled with funny people. I'd gotten into a conversation with a woman in the audience and she joined me at my table. After we had a couple of drinks she asked me where I lived, and I told her my place was way out in Malibu. In fact, I'd probably better start heading home.

"How about a cup of coffee at my place before you head home?" she asked.

"Sure, why not?" With that we got in our cars, I followed her for a few blocks to her apartment, and she pointed to a slot where I could park my car.

Growing up in Queens, New York, we lived for a few years in an apartment building just like all the other apartment buildings in New York: a rectangular building, usually eight or more stories high. You'd walk in the front door, go to the elevator, press your floor number, exit when you arrived on your floor, then walk down the hall to your apartment. In Los Angeles, however, because the weather is pretty decent most of the time, it's common to build apartment buildings around an open courtyard. When we entered her building I was kind of surprised to pass through the lobby and end up outside again. It was a very nice place. We took the outside stairway to the third floor and entered her tastefully decorated apartment. Her Siamese cat greeted me with a low, moaning growl, which sounded like a baritone with a severe toothache. Apparently he didn't like visitors. My host made a pot of coffee and we sat around talking while the cat glared at me making indifferent noises.

My host suddenly had an idea. "You know what sounds really good at this time of night? Disney music!" Okay, yeah sure. I like Disney music as well as the next guy. Anyway, the next thing I know "When You Wish Upon a Star" is blaring through her stereo at a deafening volume. After a few minutes a guy from the apartment below yelled, "Hey, turn that thing down!" My host responded by opening the window and screaming down, "Pound salt!" Then the cat became more vocal as Disney music continued to blare. The guy downstairs was screaming, "Knock it off!", and she's screaming, out the window, "Pound salt!" (putting the punchline at the end.) It wasn't turning out to be the friendly little evening I had expected. I thanked her for the coffee and fled. I was halfway home heading up the coast toward Malibu when I realized that in my haste to get out of there I'd left my jacket behind. I didn't give it a second thought. There was no way I was going back for it.

We did six fun-filled shows in that summer replacement slot and I sang, danced, and did sketches with Michele Lee, James Farentino, Annette Funicello, Frankie Avalon, Teresa Graves, Bill Bixby, Gloria Loring, and Ted Knight. That was a pretty good representation of who was hot in TV and films in those days, and we packed a lot into six episodes.

The production design on the series was pretty clever. Rather than build a bunch of complicated sets for each show, we had scenery flats that were kind of cartoonish and had the props actually painted onto them. So if the set was a kitchen, for example, the pots, pans, spice racks, and other kitchen stuff were actually painted onto the wall. The whole thing had a certain silliness to it that added to the effect of the show. We also had a live orchestra, which was fun to work with.

The series got excellent ratings, but in the end CBS executive Fred Silverman decided to go with a sitcom as a permanent series. Abe Vigoda had played a detective on the popular series *Barney Miller*, so CBS decided to capitalize on that audience recognition by creating a spinoff series named after his character on the show *Fish*.

For all the fun I had doing that show, one of my fondest memories is something that happened after the last taping. With my four kids, a lovely friend and I drove from Los Angeles to San Francisco in a motor home, where we visited friends for a few days and continued up the coast to Canada. We stopped anywhere that looked interesting and had a blast. Every Tuesday afternoon we checked into a hotel to do laundry, have room service, and watch *The John Byner Comedy Hour* on the TV in one of our rooms. Wednesday morning, we'd be back in the motor home on our way to our next adventure. After three weeks we took a ferry across to Victoria Island off the coast of Vancouver, headed east along the Canadian border, and turned south back into the states where we headed to Reno, Nevada, and a place called Pyramid Lake, just east of the "Biggest Little City" for a week. Then, it was back to Los Angeles for my next showbiz encounter.

That motor home trip was a special and amazing experience that we still talk about today. Showbiz is great, but nothing beats time with the family.

# Chapter Nine

## *The Grand Ol' (Soap) Opry*

Radio was magic. It was called "the theater of the mind" because the listeners used their imaginations to envision the stories they were hearing. A kid could imagine the Lone Ranger and Tonto racing across the Western landscape pounding justice down on the dirty bearded villains who were tormenting honest citizens. We looked up to *Jack Armstrong, the All-American Boy*, who symbolized everything that was good about American youth. We flew with *Captain Midnight*, the former World War I aviator, who fought crime, espionage, and sabotage to keep America safe. In our imaginations each of us had our own vision of what these characters looked like and the landscapes they traveled through. (Captain Midnight's crime-fighting partner was named Ichabod Mudd, but they called him Icky. Icky Mudd. Have fun coming up with your own vision of that guy.) When some of these shows later appeared on television, they never looked quite as good as the shows we'd seen in our minds. I guess that's what made them so special.

Radio wasn't just for children, though. When I was a kid in the early '40s, before Mom had to find employment, she used to listen to soap operas on the radio while doing housework. The term "soap opera" came into being because the sponsors of these programs targeted the typically female audience that listened. Women like my mom. They knew millions of women would head to the grocery stores every week to buy laundry detergent, floor wax, toothpaste, and a multitude of other items that were part of everyday life. This was the perfect audience if you were selling Tide laundry detergent, Johnson's Wax, or Colgate toothpaste. The audience for these shows was incredibly loyal, and the advertisers knew they would be tuned in five days a week, almost without fail. In the advertising world that's about as close to a sure thing as you can get. Many of these shows eventually ended up on television and today they call them daytime dramas, but they're not fooling us. They're soap operas.

The soaps were dramas—serials—with storylines that never really ended, but rather blended together and grew more and more complex. Every episode ended with a kind of cliffhanger that left the listener anxious to tune in the next day and see what happened. Many a devoted fan would head to the telephone at the end of their favorite show to call a friend and speculate on the outcome of the current crisis. It was almost an addiction, but a safe and entertaining one. By the way, men who happened to be home during the day got every bit as hooked on these shows as the women did. They just didn't talk about it. It was kind of a guilty pleasure.

During this time we were living in a house on 225th Street in the town of Laurelton, Long Island. This was the first house I really remember living in as a kid. It was a two-story structure and Mom had things set up so she would never miss a single word of her favorite shows. We had one radio upstairs and another downstairs, both tuned to the same show, so no matter where her chores took her she was in no danger of missing one gut-wrenching moment. Gut-wrenching moments, by the way, were usually accompanied by an organ sting to make sure the audience understood the gravity of the situation.

I never appeared on a real soap opera, but I ended up on something similar that was much more to my liking. By the mid-1970s soaps had been around so long that everyone was familiar with them and pretty much everyone had an opinion about them. The devoted fans accepted them as real-life stories. Others thought the complicated plots were absolutely ridiculous. Whether they loved them or hated them, everyone was aware of them. Writer-producer Susan Harris sensed comedy gold in this genre and she created the soap opera to end all soap operas—a satirical series that she named, appropriately enough, *Soap*. The idea was to take the strange plots that were typical of daytime television and stretch them to the absurd. Like most of the daytime dramas, *Soap* revolved around one particular family, in this case, the Tates. Susan took the Tate family and their friends and launched them through an outrageous web of stories, problems, dreams, cults, relationships, and above all, strange characters. The Tate family and their friends were, well, different to say the least. They were crazy people on steroids. I was lucky enough to be one of them.

One of the recurring problems characters faced in the real soap operas was amnesia. No matter what soap opera you were listening to or watching, eventually one or more of the characters developed amnesia. I've never worked out the actual figures, but I'll bet soap opera amnesias occur ten times more than real-life amnesias. Anyway, at the beginning of season three, poor Chester Tate, played by Robert Mandan, was cruelly stricken with amnesia and disappeared. His concerned wife, Jessica Tate, played by Katherine Helmond, hired a detective to look for him. The detective, George Donahue, played by yours truly, entered the cast of crazies to take charge of the investigation. Good show, good people.

I knew it was going to be fun. However, there was one small problem. Although the show was wildly popular and I'd heard my friends talk about it, I really hadn't seen enough of it to know who played who, what was going on, and why. After all, you can't watch everything. Between the time I was hired and the time I arrived on set, there was no way to watch two years of tapes to get caught up on the plot, so I just showed up for rehearsal and hoped for the best.

It's always kind of a challenge when you guest star or come into show that's been running for a while. I suppose it's like being the new guy anywhere, except in this case for every person you meet you're actually meeting two people, the actor and the character they portray. Everyone else knows each other personally and they know their onscreen characters. I walked in knowing pretty much nothing. I hadn't met any of the cast members before, and I hadn't seen enough of the series to know how the characters interacted, so I was really flying blind. At the first table reading, and for the next few days, I was trying to sort out the complicated plot and how everyone fit into it. At first, when Detective Donahue asked a question, I didn't even know who I should be looking at. That's kind of a drawback when it comes to putting in a good performance. It was a big cast, but all of the actors were great, and I finally put the whole thing together.

Creating a new character is always interesting and exciting. The actor usually doesn't know anything about the character other than the words on the page that describe him or her, but that doesn't mean that no one has a vision of the character. The writer, the person who created the character on paper, likely has a very strong mental picture of how that character looks and acts. The director, who has the job of integrating all of the characters into the story, is also going to have a mental picture of that character. As an actor I'm going to look at those words on the page and see what mental image I come up with. Hopefully, we are all in the same general ballpark.

In the case of Detective Donahue, I was pretty much left alone to see what I could create. I based part of my character's creation on the wardrobe that was given to me. From the sport coats, shirts, and ties they provided, he struck me as a kind of soft-spoken guy, the kind of guy who fits in with the crowd more than stand out in it. I felt that played well against some of the zanier characters in the show. This is really important in an ensemble show like *Soap*. It's kind of like a jigsaw puzzle. Each character, each piece, is very different from the rest, but when you put them all together, you create something that is much more interesting than the individual parts. This all came together on dress rehearsal day, which in many ways became the most interesting day of the process for me.

Comedy is tough and unforgiving. Something is either funny or it isn't. There were things in the script that read very well but didn't necessarily play well in rehearsal. When that happened producers Tony Thomas, Paul Witt, Susan Harris, and a few of the writers would step into the situation and make changes—sometimes very simple changes, like an actor turning in a different direction or giving a character a different kind of look—and, bingo, a piece of business that seemed dead became hilarious. It takes a real special talent to recognize these situations and successfully reshape them. I watched them do this time and time again, and I was always amazed by the outcome.

Just like the real soap operas, *Soap* had plenty of complicated romantic entanglements, and I was one of them. Detective Donahue fell for Jessica Tate while he was searching for her husband, and she fell for him, too. While simultaneously searching for Chester Tate and romancing his wife, Detective Donahue got pulled into the strange vortex of the Tate family and found himself in a series of non-related chapters in the family's crazy scrapbook.

In one of the plot twists, Billy, played by Jimmy Baio, ended up in a cult and five of us decided to go rescue him. Like soldiers on a night mission, we put on black face and stealthily crept through the darkness to the compound where Billy was being held. As luck (bad luck) would have it, we ran into a guard who demanded to know what we were up to. Benson, beautifully played by Robert Guillaume, told the guard that we were a tap dancing group, the five Step Brothers. To prove we were dancers we formed a semi-circle and took turns doing a few tap moves. For my move I laid on my left side, balanced on my left arm, and shuffled my feet, making a circle on the floor. The sight of some white guys in black face impersonating a tap dance group might make some of the more politically correct uncomfortable today, but back then the whole ridiculous scene was just plain funny. There is a real art to taking a premise like that and pushing it just far enough, but not too far. The line between being farcical and being stupid is a pretty fine one. The cast and the writers on *Soap* had a magical knack for taking these bits right to the peak of comedy without tumbling over the top.

Alas, all good things come to an end, and in this case they ended when Chester Tate was found and returned safely to his family. Jessica Tate was forced to choose between her husband and me, and she chose Chester. I, as Detective Donahue, became a complete wreck, or as the British put it, "a buffoon," and went to all kinds of comedic lengths to keep from being ejected from the house by Chester, but the handwriting was on the wall, both for Detective Donahue and for me. After the table reading of the script that announced that Jessica had selected Chester, we were on a break and Susan Harris took me by the arm and whispered in my ear, "If I were Jessica, I would've chosen you." As the creator and head writer of the series, Susan could probably have done anything she wanted, but I understood what she meant. The series needed to go in a specific direction, and that direction didn't include me. I thought it was a very kind gesture on her part to acknowledge my work. I had appeared in seventeen episodes over the final two seasons of the show and really enjoyed the whole experience.

You've all probably heard stories about how difficult things can be on television or movie sets when one or more of the actors have a slight ego problem or a major personality disorder. It's not fun to perform in that kind of environment. I'm happy to say we didn't have any problems like that on *Soap*. We had a large cast that was talented and fun to be around. I'm not a particularly social guy in the sense that I never really ran around to a lot of Hollywood parties or got caught up in the industry social and networking scenes. I'm just a guy. I choose my friends because I like them, not because of who they are or what they can do for me. I enjoyed being with my fellow cast members on *Soap* and spent a little more time with some than others. For example, I always enjoyed the company of Katherine Helmond. I would frequently have lunch with her during rehearsals, and she was fun to be with and a great conversationalist. We would talk about everything, from the show, to our families, to the amount of mercury in the sushi she loved, proving that when you are with the right person, talking about anything can be fun.

Richard Mulligan was a really interesting actor to watch. His character, Burt Campbell, was frequently wild, gesturing, and semi-hysterical, but Mulligan the actor was a real artist. On Monday mornings after the first table reading we would usually grab a cup of coffee and wait while the writers, producers, and director discussed how they felt the reading had gone and what might need to be fixed. When they finished we would put the show "on its feet" and begin the rehearsal process. Mulligan couldn't wait. He was fascinating. While the rest of us knocked back a cup of coffee, he would immediately dive into his script. He would pace back and forth, mumble his lines to himself, and try out different gestures. There was nothing spontaneous about the hysterics of Burt Campbell. Richard Mulligan worked out every movement, every facial expression, and every voice inflection. He really got into his role.

I really enjoyed working with Jimmy Baio, who played Billy Tate. He was the youngest actor on the set, and probably one of the best young actors I have ever worked with. He had a great personality, was fun to work with, and was very funny.

A lot of great actors passed through the ensemble cast of *Soap*, both before and during my stint on it: Arthur Peterson Jr., Dinah Manoff, ventriloquist Jay Johnson and his dummy Bob, and Donnelly Rhodes, who would also work with me later on *Bizarre*.

One last story about *Soap* and Hollywood "glitter." On a Thursday night, about halfway through my seventeen-show run on *Soap*, I was at home making dinner for the kids and myself when I received a phone call from a guy telling me that I had won the People's Choice Award for my performance on the show. I wasn't expecting that, but it was fine with me. He told me there would be a big awards ceremony in Las Vegas the following night. I told him that I had to work on Friday taping *Soap* and asked him if they would send it to me.

"No," he said, "you have to be there in person to accept the award."

"Oh," I replied, "that's too bad, but thanks for calling."

The next morning I got to the set and there was a big crowd around Billy Crystal. I asked Jimmy Baio what was going on, and he said, "Billy has won the People's Choice Award."

"Oh," I said, "he's going to Vegas!" Jimmy asked me how I knew. "They must have gone from the Bs (Byner) to the Cs (Crystal)," I told him. When we finished taping *Soap* there was a limousine waiting to rush Billy to the airport and to Las Vegas where he could claim the award he "won."

Well, that's showbiz.

# Chapter Ten

### *A Bizarre Five Years*

Nothing stays the same; you heard it here first. (Okay, maybe you didn't hear it here first, but it's true nevertheless.) In my life I'd gone from staring at a radio, to staring at our seventeen-inch-Admiral black and white TV, to performing on black and white TV, and finally to appearing in glorious color on TV. Each of those events was a highlight in my life, but the highlights kept coming. In the '70s we started hearing a lot about something called pay TV. It was delivered by cable systems instead of over-the-air broadcast transmission, and viewers were told that for their subscription fee they would see programs free of commercials. The cable systems also offered a multitude of new channels rather than the three to six channels generally available over the air. All in all, it was a pretty exciting development. Now, I'm a performer not a technology guy. If I can do my show and people can see it, I'm happy. It doesn't really matter to me whether it goes out on the airwaves, gets piped into homes by cable, or delivered door-to-door on a DVD. On the other hand, there was no denying that cable and pay television were going to open up a lot of new opportunities. It was really just a question of when one would come my way. I didn't have to wait too long.

It was 1980 and cable subscription services were still pretty new. I had just wrapped up working on the last two seasons of *Soap* when I was contacted by producers Bob Einstein and Allan Blye, whom I had met when I guest starred on *The Sonny and Cher Show* in 1973; Bob had been one of the writers and Allan, one of the producers. *The Sonny and Cher Show* was a comedy-music series of the type that was common in the '60s and '70s. Sonny and Cher not only performed musical numbers, but traded barbed comments back and forth, with Sonny usually coming out on the short end. They were good at what they did. The rest of the show was built around guest stars, so each week had a slightly different cast. The show was popular with the audience and a lot of fun to do. Anyway, I met Bob and Alan while guesting on that show and they apparently appreciated my performance. One day the phone rang and they told me they'd like to discuss a project. Fine with me. We set up a meeting at their offices in North Hollywood.

Bob and Alan told me there was a fairly new pay-TV channel called Showtime that was looking for programming, so Bob and Alan were developing a concept they called *The Bizarre Show*. (I've been told that *Bizarre* was the first regularly scheduled show on Showtime.) They envisioned it as a sketch comedy show, but one that pushed boundaries. Because Showtime was delivered by cable and not over-the-air broadcast transmission, it was not regulated by the Federal Communications Commission for content. Language and pictures that were forbidden on broadcast television were fair game on cable. In fact, this lack of moral oversight became a selling point for the subscription-TV services. There was an audience for uncensored programming and the pay services could provide it. To give me an idea of what they had in mind they told me to envision *The Benny Hill Show*, only more so.

If you're not familiar with *The Benny Hill Show*, let me paint a picture for you. Benny Hill was a British comedian who was wildly popular not only in England, but worldwide, including a loyal audience in the United States. His show ran from 1955 to 1991, and might have gone on longer had it not gotten too expensive to produce. Much of the content was visual and slapstick in nature, and not necessarily dependent on verbal jokes that are sometimes hard to translate into other cultures and languages.

This was all well and fine, but I did have one problem with the concept. Much of *The Benny Hill Show* revolved around double entendre, sexual innuendo, and chasing scantily clad women around in a kind of modern burlesque. It was not at all the kind of thing you could do in our current politically correct world and, in fact, there were some who weren't all that happy that he was doing it then. Nevertheless, ratings talk and the show lasted for nearly four decades. But here was the problem: I'm not Benny Hill. I have always prided myself on having a very clean act. The idea of slightly dirty jokes and topless women didn't set too well with me. On the other hand, the idea of playing a multitude of different characters and working with top-flight talent as guest stars was certainly attractive. Bob and Alan assured me that this was going to be wild and crazy fun. And besides, they added, Showtime only had about one million subscribers at that time, so if it didn't work out it wasn't like that many people were going to see it.

I remembered that later when the shows were rerun on broadcast stations all over the place with the crude language bleeped and black boxes inserted over the ladies' bare breasts. I wasn't the only one caught off guard by the mass exposure. Some of the young actresses who appeared on the show had expressed concern about people—their parents, for example— seeing them topless on TV (speaking of exposure). They had also been told that not many people would see the shows. Surprise!

Despite the fact that I wasn't a hundred percent

comfortable with some of the more risqué material, Bob and Alan got one thing right: it really was wild, crazy fun. One of the great things about working in comedy is that you're always around funny people. I think there may be something I'll call a "comedy mind" that allows certain people to see the most mundane objects and circumstances in a funny way. One of the early masters of this was Stan Laurel of Laurel and Hardy fame. He could take something as simple as a step ladder and instantly turn it into a series of running gags. That's why those films endure today; everyone has a step ladder and everyone occasionally does dumb things. We relate. When you work surrounded by comedy minds you're guaranteed to spend a good portion of your workday laughing. If you don't, you better check to see if you have a pulse.

Bob, in addition to being one of the producers, was also the comedy director and a straight man in some of the sketches. The writers were all great and produced funny material. When the scripts got to us Bob and I would read them and see what additional ideas or nuances we could add to give the sketches a little extra polish. This was great fun for me, since I was always portraying a different character. In fact, Alan told me that over the course of its five-year run I had performed 350 different characters. Each time a script came in I got a chance to think about that new character and what I could bring to it with my specific abilities and my own comedy mind. Spending your days coming up with goofy ideas is not a bad way to earn a living.

Alan Blye and his brother Gary, who ran the business end of things, are Canadian, which opened up another opportunity for us. The Canadian government has been good about offering financial inducements for production companies to produce their programs and films in Canada. The production company is required to hire a majority of Canadian labor, so the policy benefits Canada by employing their talented workers and attracting foreign money. The various financial breaks allow production companies to stretch their budgets, which is always welcome. I've done many, many shows in Canada, such as *The Bobby Vinton Show*, cohosted with Alan Hamel on his show for a week, appeared on a Halloween special with Shari Lewis and Lambchop, and many more. And, of course, I did a long series of personal appearances from nightclubs to fairs north of the border. At one point my name even appeared on a list of Canadian actors. It might still be there for all I know. Rodney Dangerfield saw my name on that list and contacted me about a movie he was doing in Canada called *My Five Wives*. When I told him I wasn't Canadian, he said, "Okay, well come up to Vancouver anyway." (They hired local actors as Rodney's costars. A few weeks into the shoot I was having a cup of coffee with Rodney and he was looking kind of glum. I asked him what the problem was and he said, "None of my wives can act.") I did so many Canadian productions that to this day many fans still think I'm Canadian. Several years ago I came up with a new nationality for myself: I tell people I am a Canerican.

Back to *Bizarre*. We got things rolling by shooting a few preliminary bits in Los Angeles, but after that we were off to Toronto for ten weeks every summer. We didn't shoot entire shows at one time, but instead we shot all of the sketches independently, which were then edited and pieced into twenty-five-minute shows later. This allowed the producers to condense the amount of expensive stage and crew time by about half compared to your average sitcom. It worked out well for me, too, since all of my performances were shot in a relatively short amount of time, giving me the rest of the year to work on other projects or spend time with my family.

One of the great things about working on a sketch comedy show is that each week is different and you never know what you're going to be. I loved doing *Soap*, where I played Detective Donahue every week, but on *Bizarre*, I got to create more than one new character on every show. Maybe some actors would view that as a burden, but I think most of us in the comedy world appreciate it as a real challenge. I think comedians are held to a stricter standard than actors who perform strictly in dramas. I'm not diminishing their work at all, but the fact of the matter is, if you're supposed to be funny and you're not, everybody knows it right away. You rarely hear of an actor being accused of not being dramatic enough. As I worked on my characters, alone or with Bob, I was always aware that the audience is the ultimate judge of our success, and we were going to know their verdict immediately. When you're expecting laughs and they aren't there, it's disheartening to say the least. Fortunately, the writing on *Bizarre* was really good and we all worked hard to make certain every show was wild, crazy fun.

Comedy frequently involves poking fun at people or concepts, and on *Bizarre* we took shots at everyone and everything. We took on faith healers, presidents, other shows, dirty old men, bigots, smoking and non-smoking sections in restaurants—we had a restaurant pig section, for people who like to eat with pigs, and we used live pigs, of course actors, movies . . . you name it, it was a target. When you are successful at something you can expect others to follow your lead. That was the case with some of our material. For example, Bob Einstein was an actual producer on the show, but he also portrayed the character of my producer on camera. Our supposedly backstage conversations after the show were incorporated into the show. This turned up later on other shows such as the *It's Garry Shandling's Show*, where Rip Torn played Garry's producer and they engaged in backstage chatter and chastising. We had another bit called "Talking T-shirts" that turned up on other shows later. It was a takeoff on T-shirts with messages on them, and in the sketches an actress and I would communicate with each other through a series of messages on our shirts. Being copied isn't all that bad—after all, no one copies failure.

One of the potential pitfalls of lampooning people is that not everyone appreciates humor. The goal is to base a bit on a kernel of truth and then stretch it to the point of being outrageous for the sake of a laugh. Even though everything we did was done in fun, it wasn't always well received. One episode stands out that was actually frightening. In 1979 a group of students seized the United States embassy in Iran and held our diplomats hostage. The new religious leader of Iran, Ayatollah Khomeini, supported the movement and took to radio, television, and print media to denounce the United States. With his long gray beard, stern expression, and constant threats, Ayatollah Khomeini became an instant bogeyman in world opinion. To the comedy mind a character like that is the perfect target for a comedy sketch. *What can we do with this dark, menacing, threatening character?* we thought. *How about making him a tire salesman?* Perfect.

Months after the Ayatollah sketch aired, I was sitting in the American Airlines waiting area at the Los Angeles International Airport waiting for my kids to come in on a flight from New York. I'd gotten there early to make sure that they and the escorting airline steward would see me right when they got off the plane. With pretty much nothing to do, I pulled my hat down over my eyes, stretched my legs out, and did my best impression of a guy trying to get some rest.

I was reasonably comfortable when suddenly I felt someone kick my feet. I jolted upright and was confronted by three men who looked like they might be airline crew members. They were identically dressed in black trousers and shoes and white shirts and were obviously unhappy. They moved in close around me and one leaned into my face and snarled, "You made fun of the Ayatollah, and I should *kill* you . . . but I won't!" With that they grunted obscenities and walked toward a gate.

I have to admit that being bounced out of my peaceful thoughts by having strangers threaten my life caught me off guard. It was kind of like an electrical shock coming out of nowhere. It took a few seconds for my heart rate to drop back down, but I understood the situation. Clearly, these guys lacked a sense of humor. In the next couple of minutes the whole situation reversed again. I went from being a potential political murder target back to being a dad as the kids got off the airplane with coloring books, crayons, pilot's wings, and all the other things the airplane stewards had loaded them up with. Angry threats one minute and happy children's laughter the next. Life's emotional roller coaster.

I really enjoyed working in Toronto. The weather in the summers was great and I always had a lot of fun in that city when we weren't shooting. I also enjoyed working with the Canadian crews. We had a cue-card guy by the name of George who I will never forget. Because we were constantly fiddling with the scripts to make them funnier, and we would shoot multiple sketches in one day, it was pretty much impossible to find the time to memorize all the dialogue. That's where George came in. He would stand by with his large white cards and fat marking pens and make changes on the cue cards as fast as we could come up with new ideas. He could really blaze through those cards. In fact, I began to wonder if there wasn't something in the marking pen fumes that was acting as a stimulant. On a personal level, George had one characteristic that I absolutely loved: he was the world's best audience. George had a great sense of humor and he would rock with laughter at the zaniness when we were shooting. I was amazed that he didn't drop the cue cards. It was impossible not to notice George in hysterics out of the corner of my eye when I was performing, and I think I ended up working harder just to see how big a laugh I could get out of him.

When you're working on a crazy show like *Bizarre* it's hard to control your own laughter. It's not just that you don't want to break up and ruin the scene. Sometimes a laugh at the wrong moment can border on being dangerous. Many of the sketches we did were very physical and sometimes a stuntman was employed to do something extreme like pick me up and throw me through a breakaway wall. This could turn up in a wrestling sketch, or something like a cowboy sketch where I would be picked up and thrown through the saloon wall. Getting thrown through the wall was exciting enough for me, but there was usually a little something extra going on that the audience never knew. The man hired to throw me through walls, or whatever other abuse was in the script, was Canadian wrestler Reggie Love. He was a towering hulk of muscle, but all that bulk concealed a strong funny bone. Sometimes the sketches would get to him and I could feel him trembling as he suppressed a laugh while holding me over his head waiting for the cue to throw me. I expected to be dropped on the hard stage floor when that happened, but Reggie always held on. I'll always be grateful for that.

The Canadian actors were terrific, too. I became good friends with one of them, Tom Harvey, who frequently worked on the show. He was great at playing an Ed McMann–type sidekick on our talk show take-offs like *The KKK Talk Show*, or as the frustrated interviewer in my Johnny Cash take-off character called Johnny Bucks. Tom was always a pro and a good sport when the joke was on him. He and his wife, Bobbi, would have the whole show gang over once or twice a season for a barbecue in their yard, and we just had a great time.

And of course we brought a lot of actors and comics up from the States. Over the five-year run of the show we had some of the top names from above and below the border like Jayne Eastwood, who played my wife in many sketches, Andrea Martin, Kate Lynch, Saul Rubinek, Donnelly Rhodes, Mike Myers, Don Lake, Dave Thomas, Mark Weiner, Jack Duffy, Barry Flatman, Ken James, and Billy Van. A ton of talent . . . but wait, there's more . . . Howie Mandel, The Unknown Comic (Murray Langston), Victoria Jackson, Henny Youngman, and Pat Morita.

There were a couple other stars on the show whose names you might not recognize but whose work you enjoyed: Orin Stonebridge, the master of wardrobe who helped create the look for hundreds of characters, and Gary Chowen, my hairdresser and wig procurer who also got me into character. Gary had an interesting career, having created hairstyles for Cher since he was sixteen years old. Gary would occasionally also appear in sketches, and we remain friends to this day.

Working with actors is one thing, because we rehearse and know exactly what to expect from one another. Working with animals can be more of a crapshoot. We used animals once in a while on *Bizarre* and they were always well trained, but that was no guarantee that everything was going to work exactly right. They have minds of their own, and sometimes they let us know it. We did a circus sketch one time that called for me to follow a chimp into a waiting limousine. The chimp was wearing a tuxedo closed with Velcro. The gag was that as the chimp stepped into the limo I was to grab the jacket, which would breakaway, and pull off. At that point we would stop tape, replace the chimp with my buddy, little-person actor Billy Barty, and then pick up the scene. Once edited, as I ripped off the jacket the chimp would miraculously turn into Billy Barty.

The chimp, the trainer, and I rehearsed the scene several times and it was working out nicely. The chimp and I were getting on pretty well together. I was confident and hoped the chimp was, too. Anyway, I was supposed to be dressed in a circus ringmaster costume, so I went back to my dressing room to get into my wardrobe while the audience was let into the studio. At that point Bob Einstein showed up. He had been off the set doing interviews and missed the rehearsal, so he asked me to run the scene one more time with the chimp so he could see it. It was only about twenty minutes to show time, but I got ready and went out to do it again.

I was in costume and ready, the chimp was in his suit and ready, and the trainer was standing by and ready. We stepped out into the hall to rehearse out of sight of the audience and ran the scene as before. This time, however, when I went to pull the jacket off of him some of the chimp's hair had been caught in the Velcro and it hurt him. He turned around, grabbed my lower lip, and twisted it until blood squirted out. I'm guessing the lip squeeze was the trainer's way of punishing him when he did something wrong, so this is how the chimp explained to me that I had done something wrong. It was ten minutes to show time and I'd been reprimanded by a chimp and I was dribbling blood all over the hallway.

"No problem," the trainer said. "I have some aloe that I can put on your lip and it will stop the bleeding right away." The trainer was prepared; apparently I wasn't the chimp's first victim. For the next ten minutes I applied layer after layer of aloe on my lip, and by the miraculous healing power of the plant it worked. The trainer redressed the chimp, more carefully this time, and the sketch went off with no further problems or injuries.

On another occasion the trainer used a cute little black and white monkey that was about seven inches tall. In the sketch I was a blind man wearing dark glasses with an old-fashioned music grinder. The monkey sat on the grinder as I went from apartment to apartment, knocking on doors and telling whoever answered that I was collecting money for something or other. When we reached a specific door a beautiful young woman, wrapped in a towel as though fresh from the shower, answered the door. I identified myself as a blind man collecting money, and as she reached for her purse the towel slipped revealing her breasts. I collected the money, she closed the door, I took a few steps away, then returned to the door and knocked again. When she answered I asked, "Can you do that again?" She slammed the door in my face. Fairly simple.

We rehearsed. The problem arose when the monkey wasn't interested in anything else except the sunglasses I was wearing. She could see her reflection in the lenses and she was fascinated by it. She kept climbing up and staring at herself in my shades, nose to nose. The trainer couldn't get the monkey to stop doing it, and I couldn't get comfortable with a monkey in my face. I finally told Bob that I wasn't going to be able to do this, so Bob decided to replace me with the trainer. When the woman opened the door the camera would be on her anyway, so he figured it would work. Great. So the trainer got in my costume. The actress was in her towel and the monkey was behaving. When it got to the point in the sketch where the woman handed over the money, the monkey suddenly got jealous of the woman reaching out to the trainer. Annoyed, the little thing jumped on the woman and bit her right on her left nipple. Naturally, the actress was pretty upset over that and the rest of us just kind of stood there in shock. The next day the actress's very large boyfriend showed up to discuss the whole thing with Bob. Ah, the joys of working with animals.

There was one sketch on *Bizarre* that ended up taking on a life of its own. It was based on a character Bob had performed once on *The Dick Van Dyke Show* years earlier, and Bob and Allan decided to reintroduce the character on *Bizarre*. Little did I know that this was the beginning of their shaping that character to eventually spin off into its own show. That character was called Super Dave Osborne, and he was basically the world's worst daredevil. He was a parody of Evel Knievel, except that nothing he did ever worked out as planned. Bob, as Super Dave, dressed in a red-white-and-blue outfit, gloves, boots, and helmet, would introduce a stunt with great bravado and confidence, only to have everything pretty much go to hell when he attempted it. Standing next to him was his Japanese assistant, Fuji, played by Art Irizawa, who became the brunt of Super Dave's frustration. Once Super Dave's ego was deflated by failure he would turn to Fuji and blame everything on him with comments like, "Now I know why you guys lost the war." And much worse. The absurdity of the whole thing clicked with audiences, particularly the college crowd. After the final *Bizarre* taping at the end of the fifth season Bob turned to me and said, "I think I've had enough of *Bizarre*. How about you?" I figured if that's the way it's going to be, that's the way it's going to be. *Bizarre* was over, but Bob and Allan launched a new series based on Super Dave.

To this day I receive fan mail and messages from fans who love *Bizarre* and wish it were still on the air. I have to admit that I had at least as much fun making that series as they had watching. Sometimes things just work out for everyone. Although it's been off the air for years, episodes of *Bizarre* are available for purchase on websites like Amazon. I've also seen some of the sketches on YouTube. I don't make a nickel from any of those DVD sales or from YouTube, but I want to let the loyal audience know that they're out there. There's no reason for the laughs to stop now.

# Chapter Eleven

## *The "King" and Mr. Fonda*

Everybody has to start somewhere and each one of us has our own unique beginning. While I was a young sailor doing impressions for the crew of a submarine, an exciting young singer was starting to get some attention cutting 45 rpm singles for Sun Records in Memphis, Tennessee. (If you don't know what a 45 rpm single is, ask your grandparents.) He had a name I'd never heard before—Elvis—and when he sang he threw his whole body into the act. By the time I was discharged from the navy, Elvis had become a huge success. In a classic case of bad timing, this was also the point where Elvis was drafted into the army. Some people felt being out of the public eye for two years would kill his career. Boy, were they wrong. Pictures of Elvis in uniform filled the pages of fan magazines and he became more popular than ever. When his two-year hitch was up he went back to cutting records, performing concerts, and acting in movies. He was unstoppable.

Elvis eventually earned the title the King of Rock 'n' Roll, or just The King. Both were correct. He was unchallenged for the throne of rock 'n' roll singers, but he was more than that. He symbolized the beginning of a revolution in music and youth that propelled America from the sedate 1950s into an era of change, both musical and social. From the moment he thrust his pelvis into American pop culture on *The Jimmy Dorsey Show* in 1956 (which I watched as a sailor aboard the USS *Florikan*) until his premature death at Graceland in 1977, he was the one and only undisputed king and there were no challengers. On records, in movies, and in concert he made many millions look and listen. He was a phenomenon. When Elvis took the stage he was bigger than life, and that made him the perfect subject for an impersonation. Elvis was a part of my act for years before I actually met him.

Some people think that everyone in show business knows one another, that we spend our weekends hanging out flying off to exotic destinations for fabulous parties. Not true. In some ways being an entertainer is little different from being a traveling salesman. You make a lot of friends in a lot of different places and get a lot of frequent flyer miles. You have to go a long way before you get anywhere. Who you meet depends on where you go and who you work with. As you climb the celebrity ladder the names get bigger, but very few performers start at the top. The climb may be brief or lengthy, but there's going to be a climb.

Like most performers, I didn't start out associating with the Elvis Presleys of the business. Sure, we both had our names on Las Vegas hotel marquees, but his was in much, much bigger letters. They used to say that when the letters of your name on the marquee were bigger than the words "Shrimp Cocktail" you knew you were on your way. When I first met Elvis I certainly wasn't being out-billed by seafood—I was starring on Vegas stages, after all—but Elvis was a Vegas legend. He still is.

As you can imagine, my first meeting with him was memorable. Sort of. It was also at the old Hilton International Hotel. After my show I decided to head for the casino and fan some money through the one-armed bandits. As I walked across the crowded gaming space, I heard some excitement coming from the craps tables. I looked over and there he was,

The King with his court (commonly known as the Memphis Mafia) crowded around him. As I passed, he looked into the casino and spotted me.

"Hey, John," he shouted over the din.

"How's it going?" I shouted back.

"Down the tubes," he said, indicating the dice table.

That was it. That was the whole thing. Elvis had acknowledged me and I had acknowledged him. It was a nice, friendly interchange with The King, but hardly what you would call a bonding experience. I continued on to the slot machines, made a modest investment in silver dollars, and tried my luck. Five or six minutes later one of the guys from Elvis's entourage walked up to me and introduced himself. He told me Elvis and the guys liked to laugh—in fact, that's how he got on Elvis's payroll. He was a comedian of sorts, and it was his job to keep Elvis and the boys laughing. I commented that it was nice to hear that Elvis liked to laugh, that the guy had a pretty good job, and some other things of that type that you say when you're making small talk with someone you don't know. After a few minutes Elvis's court jester said goodbye and returned to his spot among Elvis's crew. I thought it was kind of interesting that Elvis had his own personal comedian. Several years later I heard that this guy stole some jewelry from Elvis and Elvis had to race to the airport to get it back before the guy left town. My guess is that Elvis didn't think that was funny.

As I continued to work Las Vegas there continued to be Elvis sightings. Apparently, he liked seeing a good show as well as he liked giving one. I was working at the Frontier Hotel with Diana Ross, perhaps the top female vocalist of her time. The shows were packed. As I mentioned, Elvis impressions had been a staple of my act since I was performing for my buddies on our ship in the navy. They were always popular with audiences, so I never had any reason to stop doing them. Elvis had a distinct style, and a distinct style is prime fodder for exaggerating into humor. My television appearances on *The Ed Sullivan Show* and *The Tonight Show starring Johnny Carson* brought my Elvis impersonation into living rooms across the country, so when audiences bought a ticket to my show in Las Vegas, they expected to see it. I loved doing it, so that worked out well for everyone.

I never launch directly into an impression. I like to start by talking a bit about the person I'm about to do, usually by making a few jokes about their style or character. Elvis was a mover. He seemed to have more moving parts than the average human being and he used all of them. When he took the stage he took all of it, moving back and forth to the rhythm of his music. In my lead-up to the impression, I mentioned that Elvis paced the stage like a caged animal. During a show one night I didn't get much further than that when a guy in the front row yelled at me.

"Why don't you get him up on stage?!" That probably wasn't the dumbest question I had ever heard come from an alcohol-fueled audience member, but it belonged in the top ten.

"Yeah," I said sarcastically, "he's waiting in the wings in case someone like you tells me to bring him out."

"No, seriously. He's in the house!" the guy shouted, pointing to the back of the showroom.

Sure enough, the follow spots swung around and illuminated a booth in the back of the room where Elvis was encamped with his boys. I wasn't expecting that, so I didn't have a quick response to the situation. Elvis stood and acknowledged the audience.

"Hey, we love you, Elvis," I shouted. "I've got a couple of minutes, do you want to come up and have a few laughs?" He motioned that he had to leave, and he and the boys headed for the door. Obviously, he had wanted to see Diana and me perform, but he didn't want to be a distraction so he slipped out. That was courteous, but unfortunate.

On July 17, 1970, I was playing at the Hilton International in Las Vegas in a show with Glen Campbell and we were having a pretty good time. Good audiences, lots of laughs, no complaints. When you're booked into a show, you don't get to take days and nights off for family obligations. My daughter Sandra's tenth birthday was going to fall during this gig, and there was no chance of me heading back to Malibu for a birthday party, so we decided to have it in Las Vegas. Normally they don't let children in the showroom, but we did a clean show and it was a special night for her, so the hotel let her and her sister, Rosine, age eight, and brother Don, age six, sit in the balcony, first row center. My other daughter, Patricia, age four, was at home. I finished my act, and as I reached the balcony to join the kids, I heard Glen announce that Elvis was in the audience. Thunderous applause. The spotlights swung around and there he was, in a main floor booth directly below us. The applause died, the lights dimmed, and Glen began to sing. Suddenly I got the feeling that something wasn't quite right. I looked around in the semi-darkness and noticed that the birthday girl was missing.

"Where's Sandi?" I asked.

"Look down there," Don answered, pointing to the booth below. There was Sandi, standing in the aisle talking to The King. It was kind of cute, Elvis talking to the beaming ten-year-old fan. But she didn't come back. I looked down again and there she was sitting in Elvis's lap. Kid moves fast.

When the show was over I saw Sandi, escorted by Elvis and his entourage, heading back to Glen's dressing room, so I took Rosine and Don back to our suite and then headed down to the dressing rooms to collect my starstruck daughter. Unbeknownst to me, Sandi had paid her respects to Glen, had her picture taken with Elvis, and was already on her way back to our suite.

I went downstairs to cross through the kitchen that led to the stairway to my dressing room. After dodging cooks and waiters in the hot kitchen (part of the glamour of show business) I made it to the stairway. There, suddenly filling the doorway was The King, flanked by the Memphis Mafia, coming back from Glen's dressing room. In his elegant outfit, black with a white shirt, pink neckerchief with black accents, and a turquoise and silver belt, he could not have looked more regal. As I stepped in front of him, he stared at me straight faced with his arms at his sides. After a quiet moment or two I said, "Hi Elvis," through a big smile and reached out and lifted his limp hand to shake it. It was like shaking nothing. When I released his hand, he said to me in that slow, Southern draw, "I pace like a caged animal, huh?"

I wasn't expecting that. He gave me a frigid look and then walked past. The Memphis Mafia also gave me a collective frigid look as they walked past quickly to stay in the aura of his glory. Apparently, I had offended The King. Off with my head.

I didn't mean to offend Elvis. In fact, I've never meant to offend anyone. But I'm a comic, and comics tell jokes. That's what we do. In my case, I'm an impressionist. I take people who are already larger than life and further inflate them for the sake of a laugh. The things I say about my peers I say respectfully for the sake of good fun. Apparently what they hear, as in the case of Elvis, may be something else. I would never deliberately insult anyone, unlike my late pal Don Rickles did. He was the undisputed master of insult comedy, cutting down the high and mighty, but in a hilarious way that had them coming back for more. A scar from the razor-sharp tongue of Don was considered a badge of honor. But that was Don's style, not mine.

I was feeling pretty good about things until I bumped into Elvis, but his attitude put a real damper on my mood. I just stood there for a moment. Have you ever gotten that little feeling in your heart when you realize you've been misunderstood and accidentally insulted someone? I felt bad. Then I heard that familiar voice again.

"Hey John," Elvis said as I turned to face him. "I met your daughter Sandi. She's real nice." He was laughing and so were his guys. He'd been putting me on. The King really did like a laugh, and this time the laugh was on me.

A few years later I was working with singer-songwriter Bobbie Gentry in a show that was about music through the years. In the show I impersonated singers from the '40s on up through the '50s: Nat King Cole, Perry Como, Tony Bennett, and Frank Sinatra from the '40s, and Little Richard, Bill Haley, Johnny Mathis, and a few others from the '50s. Bobbie sang her hits "Ode to Billy Joe," "Fancy," "Don't Let Me Down," and big production number "Heartbreak Hotel." We were booked into some very popular hotel-casino showrooms for weeks at a time, moving from the Desert Inn in Las Vegas, to Harrah's in Reno, and a return to Las Vegas at the Frontier Hotel. That's where Elvis came back into my life.

In the Frontier, my dressing room was downstairs from the stage, while Bobbie's was a house trailer just off stage right, where she could make quick changes. While in Vegas I would get into my car between shows and drive out to the desert, roll the windows down, listen to a bit of radio, and breathe the fresh air. It was the perfect break from performing in front of hundreds of people in a smoke-filled showroom. When I'd return to my dressing room my new friend, Eddie Ponder, the drummer with the band Bobbie had assembled for the shows, would always be there, and he told me that on several occasions Elvis had stopped by looking for me.

One night after the last show Ed and I were in the dressing room talking about grabbing a bite to eat when my phone rang. It was Bobbie calling from the trailer telling me that there was someone there who wanted to see me. I went upstairs to stage right and the trailer, knocked on her door, and Elvis, wearing a black outfit, matching cowboy hat, and big smile, opened it. He immediately apologized for wearing the hat, telling me that he was having "a bad hair day." We sat across from each other, he on a chair, me on a sofa. At one point he excused himself, went into another part of the trailer, and upon returning, leaned over the couch in back of me and asked if I and a few of my friends would like to come over to the Hilton and hang out for a bit. I said okay and returned to my room to invite Ed and my manager, Harry, to join me. Off we went.

The three of us drove over to the hotel and walked to the bank of elevators that went to Elvis's suite. I gave my name to the security guard and he immediately opened the doors and let us go up. Elvis's suite was enormous, rooms of furniture, paintings, a courtyard, and on and on. The Memphis Mafia was there as was his doctor, a young guy in a beautiful white suit. After the introductions were complete, Elvis put his right arm over my shoulders and led me to a console phonograph while telling me that he was excited to have been bumped up to having "fifty-one percent of himself," which now gave him complete control over his choices in life. Prior to this, Colonel Tom Parker had 51 percent to Elvis's 49 percent.

When we got to the record player he said that he had just finished recording a song that he would like to play for me. We sat cross-legged on the floor in front of the player and listened to the record many times. Each time he wanted to hear it again he'd make an effort to replay it, but he would always have to call his friend and assistant Red West, who was in charge of all things mechanical, to do it for him. The working title of the song was "Born to Rock 'n' Roll." I liked it a lot and I didn't mind hearing it several times.

At the end of the listening, he summoned his doctor and announced to me as he headed toward one of the many bedrooms, "John, I'm going to get a vitamin shot between my toes. Do you want to come and watch?" I decided I didn't need to do that, so instead I took a tour of the palatial suite. When I worked my way back, there was Elvis completing a demonstration of some karate moves he and Red had worked out. It was a scene that Elvis called "how to defend against someone with a loaded pistol pointed at you" and I arrived just as it was ending. Elvis was pointing the pistol at Red who was on his knees with hands folded as though praying when I quipped, "Aw, leave him alone, Elvis, he just wants to know where the bathroom is." Elvis replied, "Bathroom, that's cute."

The night was far from over. Elvis and the boys gathered around the piano to sing gospel songs, kind of a private concert for his friends. Near dawn there were small groups of people in different areas of the vast room. Elvis was seated in a corner by himself when I approached him. He stood and I thanked him for the evening, and while shaking hands I told him that he was a living legend.

"I never thought of it that way," he said.

The three of us said our goodnights and tiptoed out. That was the last I would see him. A few years later I was being made up for a scene when the makeup man asked if I had heard about Elvis. It was a shock to say the least. Gone too soon, forty-two years old. The King is dead. Long live his memory.

I guess we all have our personal heroes, people we admire, or just famous people we'd like to meet. One of the great things about being in show business for me was that I got to meet some of the people I'd seen on those giant theater screens when I was a kid. One of the biggies was Henry Fonda. Fonda had had a long, successful career in Hollywood and appeared in many popular movies of my youth such as *Young Mr. Lincoln*, *Drums Along the Mohawk*, *The Grapes of Wrath*, and *The Return of Frank James*. Fonda was a film legend when I was still a kid, so the thought of not only meeting him but actually working with him was pretty exciting. Of course, things didn't start out exactly as I expected.

In the fall of 1977, I was flown to an airport outside of the town of Oroville, in Northern California. I don't know exactly what happened—if it was deliberately scheduled this way, or if something unexpected had come up—but when I landed I was quickly escorted to a car that was standing ready for me at the airport. Everyone was in a big hurry to take me directly to the set. There wasn't going to be your typical meet-and-greet with the rest of the cast and director over dinner or cocktails. I was going to work. Right then. I'm not big on dinners and parties anyway, but it really does help if you have a little time to get into the proper mindset of what you're about to do. In this case, my body was being rushed to the set and my mindset would have to catch up.

The picture we were about to make was called *The Last of the Cowboys*, and also later known as *The Great Smokey Roadblock*. It's the story of a long-haul truck driver named Elegant John Howard, played by Fonda, who had a long, spotless, safe career at the wheel, but failing health was forcing him to give up the road. He wasn't happy about leaving the career he enjoyed so much, so he decided to go out with a bang by making one more run. Step one was stealing his truck from an impound lot. That kind of gives you a feeling of where the movie went from there.

I played a disc jockey by the name of Bobby Apples who popped up throughout the story. Eileen Brennan was the female lead and the rest of the cast was made up of some first-class actors: Susan Sarandon, Dub Taylor, and Austin Pendleton, just to name a few. Henry Fonda was about seventy-two years old when he made this film and was perfect as the crusty truck driver. I was really looking forward to working with him.

Meanwhile, back in the car speeding to the set, we raced off through the night until we reached a rural, wooded area, pitch black. (I've never been kidnapped, but I imagine it's probably something like this.) Once we reached the middle of nowhere, my escorts/captors led me through the darkness to a pool of light created by the movie lights, where I met writer-director John Leone, who quickly introduced me to his staff. One of them pushed the script into my hand, turned it to the correct page, and led me to a seat on the ground where I looked up at the windshield of an enormous Mack truck. They would only be using my voice in this shot, so I didn't need wardrobe or makeup. That was good, since the way things were going they might have tried to do them in the car.

As I sat in my seat the assistant stood behind me holding a flashlight on the script so I could read it and then pointed up at the driver's window, which was on about a forty-five-degree angle. As the film lights came up I could see Henry Fonda in the driver's seat with Eileen Brennan sitting next to him. From where I was seated they looked like two head shots on a Mack truck windshield. The assistant director called for the camera to roll, the assistant held the flashlight steadily, and I looked up at Fonda and Brennan as I delivered the lines that they were supposedly hearing on the radio. Prop assistants passed tree branches in front of the lights to throw shadows on the truck that made it look like it was moving through the moonlight. I'd never seen that before and I found it interesting, but I had to focus on what I was doing.

After my last take the assistants quickly found me and hustled me off to the hotel where I would be quartered for the next few weeks. I had just managed to work with Henry Fonda and Eileen Brennan without actually meeting them. Only in Hollywood. (Or Oroville.)

I didn't get to meet Mr. Fonda until about three days later. He looked, walked, and talked exactly like Henry Fonda. That may seem like an odd statement, but not everyone or everything is as it appears in the movies. However, in the case of Mr. Fonda, what you saw on the screen was what you got in real life, at least from my experience. I have to admit that I was excited. I'm always surprised when a great star such as him turns out to be a regular, good guy.

My enthusiasm got some unwanted attention one night when we were having dinner. There were basically just two restaurants near our location, so at dinnertime the cast and crew were in one or the other, most sitting in small groups. When I walked in I saw Mr. Fonda and his wife, Shirlee, sitting alone at a table, and they waved at me to join them. This was not the kind of old-fashioned Hollywood dinner at Chasen's that they used to write about in the fan magazines. It was more like a bunch of working people in a coffee shop creating the kind of din one finds in such places. There was even music from a jukebox.

I hadn't yet had the chance to tell him what it meant to me to be working with him, so I figured this was the moment with just three of us at the table. I said, "Mr. Fonda, it's an honor to be working with you." I hadn't worked with him long enough to realize that he had a significant hearing problem.

"*What?*" he shouted back.

I boosted my volume. *"It's an honor to be working with you!"* I shouted. Unfortunately, just as I began to yell my compliment the jukebox abruptly stopped. Everyone in the place turned to look at me to see what the shouting was about. It was a little embarrassing, but I'm sure they were all honored to be working with him, too. They just didn't yell it out in restaurants. (The shouting incident in the restaurant reminds me of something that happened years earlier on a flight from Las Vegas to Los Angeles. I slid into an aisle seat next to an eleven- or twelve-year-old girl who was sitting at the window. I politely said hello and we had a conversation, much of it dealing with the fact that her parents were divorced and had joint custody. Her father lived in Las Vegas and her mother lived in Los Angeles, so she was a frequent flyer on this route. She confessed that she was happy to be returning to Los Angeles, since she much preferred to live with her mother. So I said loudly over the noise of the engines, "Then why don't you stay with your mother?" She responded even more loudly, "*What would my father say?!*" But just before she replied, the engines stopped. Everyone on the plane looked at me, wondering what I'd said to that young girl to make her yell that response. Sometimes you can't win.)

The movie shoot in Oroville continued very well and the weather was perfect. There was enough time between scenes and shots for Mr. Fonda and me to spend some time watching the salmon swim and jump upstream in the river, and wander down the riverbank looking for bits of fool's gold. It wasn't the kind of thing I ever would have dreamed of doing with an iconic movie star and I enjoyed every minute of it.

When you're on a film every day the director, producer, cinematographer, and sometimes the stars and other key people, find time to look at "dailies." Dailies are the printed takes from the previous day's shooting. In the days when everyone shot on film they would only print the takes that the director felt were good. The key people would gather to watch dailies to make sure they were happy with the product and would immediately go back and reshoot if they didn't like what they saw. We were watching dailies one night with me sitting on Mr. Fonda's left and his wife, Shirlee, on his right. Apparently, Mr. Fonda was on a pretty strict no-salt diet, and Shirlee was the one who enforced it. As we sat in the dark I noticed that every few minutes Mr. Fonda would carefully and slowly lift his left hand to his left shirt pocket, remove one popcorn kernel, then slowly bring it up the side of his neck to the corner of his mouth and sneak it in. Shirlee never knew. I guess it made Mr. Fonda feel as though he'd really been to the movies.

Working with Hollywood legends like Henry Fonda always reminded me of my parents. Mom and Dad were fans of many of the legendary performers that I worked with over the years. It was always kind of special working with someone who I knew my parents had enjoyed watching on the big screen years, or decades, before. As a kid my first impersonation was of Bing Crosby, and I eventually worked with Bing many times. In the '30s and '40s there were few people who were more popular and talented than Fred Astaire, and my parents were fans. I worked with him in the TV movie *The Man in the Santa Claus Suit*. He was a great guy. I was fortunate to number Sid Caesar among my close friends. He lit up our living room on the mighty, seventeen-inch Admiral during the early years of television, and decades later we would spend many hours laughing together.

I knew Cyd Charisse from the Friars Club in Los Angeles. When I would run into her at some Hollywood affair, Cyd would always ask, "Are you going to perform tonight?" We were fans of each other. Her husband, Tony Martin, was a performer my mother absolutely loved. While we were living in Bohemia, Long Island, somewhere around 1948, I can recall one day when Dad was working on his '32 Chevrolet. He pulled the engine out and had it literally spread out on the lawn. My mother, who had been working in the house, came to the window and told him that there was a movie theater in Islip, a few towns to the west of us, that was showing a Tony Martin movie and she wanted to see it. Dad, the dutiful husband and master mechanic, had the engine put together and back in the car in an hour and a half, plenty of time to load us all in the car and make it into the theater before the lights dimmed. I told that story years later at an affair honoring Tony. That was a special moment.

Bob Hope was another family favorite I worked with, as well as Ray Bolger. I appeared with June Allyson in *Three on a Date*, another made-for-TV movie. I appeared with Jack Benny on *The Garry Moore Show* in 1966, and James Cagney invited me to his home twice. On one of those occasions Donald O'Connor and I teamed up to do a rendition of "Yankee Doodle Dandy" for him, which made his night.

So many great memories. I'm happy and proud to have known them all.

# Chapter Twelve
## *Talk the Talk*

Daytime television has always had its own unique personality. The soap operas, a holdover from radio, had an amazing ability to pull listeners and viewers into their complex stories and practically become an obsession with many people. The soaps pretty much commanded the late morning-early afternoon timeslots for decades. Once the soaps ended for the day, depending on the TV station you were watching, you might have a local station running a movie, providing local children's programming, or running a syndicated talk show.

The syndicated talk shows were great for me for a couple of reasons. First of all, there were a lot of them, which meant there were a lot of opportunities to perform. Merv Griffin and Mike Douglas had long-running talk shows with strong audiences. John Davidson had a talk show that combined his vocal talents with guest appearances by popular celebrities. Phil Donahue had a long-running show that tended to focus more on serious content rather than entertainment. Back in those days most of the talk show hosts were men, with one big exception: Dinah Shore.

Dinah Shore was the queen of afternoon talk/variety shows for many years. The afternoon slot was one of many series on her career path that included being a radio star, recording star, movie star, prime-time television star, and then a friendly afternoon hostess people loved to welcome into their homes.

A beautiful smile, a soft southern hello, a lovely singing

voice, and a wonderful cook—that was Dinah Shore. To that, add a hearty, honest laugh. She was special, but she was real. She was personal. When she would lead me into a question she would reach out and take my hand, like a caring friend. She did the same thing when she asked me for a special impersonation, which in most cases was Johnny Mathis. By 1974 I had appeared thirteen times on *The Dinah Shore Show*. The shows were all fun and memorable, but a few stand out.

One of them was with a singer I had been a fan of since I was a kid, Frankie Laine. Frankie had huge hits on the radio when I was growing up, like "Mule Train," "Cry of the Wild Goose," "Jezebel," "That's My Desire," and the theme song from the TV western *Rawhide*, to name just a few. Well, after Dinah completed her interview with Mr. Laine, she turned to her audience and said, "And now ladies and gentleman, Frankie and Johnny will sing for you!"

The song was "That's My Desire." We took turns singing lines from the song, he doing his Frankie Laine, and I doing my Frankie Laine, accompanied by Dinah's studio musicians. When we hit that last, high "that's my desire," I harmonized with him to the roar and delight of Dinah and her audience. I can't even express what it was like to perform like that with someone whose work you really respect. If there are golden moments in life, that was one.

Another thing I particularly enjoyed about doing Dinah's show was that she and her staff seemed to give more thought to assembling the guests for each episode than some of the other shows. They didn't seem to put together a show based on who was available, but rather who would work well together. As a result, she had some pretty good matchups that not only made for good entertainment, but made the show even more fun to do. For example, on one of her shows she had booked me along with a friend of mine, Richard Pryor. Richard was a truly unique talent and pal. We had known each other for years and would sometimes spend a few evenings laughing the night away at a bar called The No Name in Sausalito, California, where I lived at the time. We had never appeared on any show together before Dinah's, so we were really looking forward to this opportunity.

Unfortunately, it didn't go quite as well is it could have because of something I did that I wish I hadn't. Not the fault of Dinah or Richard, but the insecurity of my then-personal manager, Harry Colomby. I guess he thought it necessary to give me a sort of pep talk before the taping. "Now don't forget, Richard is a very funny guy, and you want be on your toes." I guess Harry felt that Richard might come on strong and kind of upstage me. Richard and I were friends and that wasn't likely to happen, but Harry had planted that seed in my mind and I responded. The show went off okay as far as I was concerned, but when I was with Richard a few months later, I mentioned the show to him and he replied, "Man, you sure were working that day, really working!" I realized that I had been, and he busted me for not being the guy he knew at that time. I am afraid I may have done to Richard exactly what Harry was afraid Richard was going to do to me.

Dinah liked for me to bring my kids to the shows, and while driving them home one night, my oldest, Sandra, age eleven at the time, told me that while I was rehearsing with the band that afternoon, Dinah said to her, "Put in a good word for me to your dad!" That made me smile. One day my kids and I were in the process of painting some things in our garage when one of them told me that we needed a few items from the grocery store. Thinking that I would just dash in and get what was needed—no need to change out of the work duds—I parked in the lot, started to head toward the store, and who was walking in my direction? Dinah and her mother, all decked out in stylish summer togs. Dinah gave me an amused look and said, "Mom, this is John Byner, a talented guy, and he cleans up pretty good!"

The last time I was in the same room with Dinah was at a tribute to singer Tony Martin at the Friars Club in Beverly Hills, California. She was introduced while seated in the audience. I intended to go over to her table when the program concluded, but I got tied up in another conversation and waited too long. When I broke free and went looking for her she had already left. An absolutely wonderful lady. I always wish I hadn't waited that night, for just a few weeks later, Dinah Shore was gone.

It was through Dinah Shore that I met Burt Reynolds. As it turned out, Burt was as big a fan of me as I was of him, so we both looked forward to the meeting. At the time Burt and Dinah were dating and in a very happy relationship. It caused a few eyebrows to raise, since Burt was twenty years younger than Dinah, but the age difference didn't seem to be a factor for either of them. I had done Dinah's show a few times before and thought I might run into him after the show, but it hadn't happened. Finally Burt and I were actually booked together on the show, so I not only met him, but got to work with him.

Two things about Burt immediately stood out as being genuine. He had a smile that was absolutely infectious. If he smiled, you were going to smile, too. You couldn't help it. The other thing was his laugh. It was a high-pitched cackle that sounded like a cross between his friend Jim Hampton and Steve Allen. Just like with his smile, if Burt laughed you were going to laugh. On that show Dinah, Burt, the audience, and I laughed a whole lot. In fact, I really don't even remember what we talked about except that we laughed and laughed and laughed. Any day like that is a good day no matter what business you're in.

As an impressionist I make a living copying other people and distorting their image for laughs. I'm not used to having people copy me, but Burt got a huge kick out of doing what I did. At one point in the show Burt and I were standing on a riser behind the couch where Dinah was sitting. At the end of our bit we were supposed to walk down the steps and sit next to her on the couch. Instead of walking down the steps I leapt over the couch, landed on my feet, and then sat down gracefully. A second later, out of the corner of my eye, I saw Burt flying through the air and make a perfect landing next to me. The audience went wild. As I said, we laughed and laughed and laughed.

A few weeks after that show, I was invited to Dinah's house for a birthday party she was hosting for Burt. As I've said before, I'm not a big Hollywood socializer, but I wouldn't have missed that party for the world. As one would expect, Dinah's house was as beautiful as her personality. It was gorgeously decorated and looked like it belonged to a happy, vibrant person. The guest list was pretty impressive as well. I can't remember everyone who was there that night, but as you can imagine, Dinah and Burt had a lot of A-list friends, and they were friends who enjoyed each other's company and liked to have a good time. It was one of those nights when you could find yourself passing a tray of hors d'oeuvres from Gene Hackman to Anne Bancroft. Very classy. I was about to accidentally put a crimp in that.

This was one of those times when you ask yourself, "What do you give to the guy who has everything?" Dinah had the solution to that. She wanted all of the gifts to be funny, which made perfect sense considering Burt's sense of humor. This was a premise I could work with, and I came up with a gag gift that I thought was pretty funny. Unfortunately, it didn't come off as planned.

In the early '70s there was a lot of talk—from college campuses to *Time* magazine— about smoking pot. It was either a blessing or curse, depending on who you talked to, but it had suddenly become a big part of our culture. My idea was to give Burt a supposed starter kit for pot smokers. I got a 4-by-4-inch box, labeled it "How to Roll a Joint," and included items with labels so the novice smoker would know what to do. There was a package of rolling papers labeled "Your Papers," a bamboo roller labeled "Your Roller," and then a small container for the product. In the language of the day, pot was frequently referred to as (excuse the expression) "shit," so the product container was labeled "Your Shit." In that container, instead of the expected substance, I put in some sun-dried manure from my horse stable. In other words, I had a very accurately labeled package. So far, so good.

We were all having a really great time when Dinah decided it was time for Burt to open his presents. At the dinner table. I was at an A-list party in Dinah Shore's beautiful house and I had given her boyfriend a package of poop that he was about to open at her exquisitely decorated dinner table. The gag gifts began. There were silly little things like a box labeled "This Man is Wanted by the Police" that held a mirror that popped up. I was hoping that they'd delay opening the rest of the gifts until after dinner, but no such luck. When my gift was opened, Burt and Dinah both held their noses and exclaimed, "That's real manure!" I felt like I wanted to crawl to the door. I got a few cold looks, but everyone got over it and took it for the joke it was meant to be.

I spent most of the rest of the night entertaining Mel Brooks and his wife, Anne Bancroft. They asked me to do some of their favorite characters, such as George Jessel and Ed Sullivan, and the laughs continued all night. Before they left Mel turned to me and said, "John, you're tops in taps," an old show business expression meaning someone is the best. Coming from a guy like Mel Brooks, that was a huge compliment.

I didn't see Burt again for several years, but we were both invited to an affair at the Beverly Hills Hotel where we had a chance to catch up. We swapped a few stories about people like John Wayne and had a few laughs, and it was a good evening. A few months later I was invited by Burt to appear in a movie he was starring in called *Stroker Ace*. He wanted me to play the part of his childhood friend, Doc Seegle, who showed up later in life to save Stroker's reputation as a stock car racing driver by convincing his sponsor not to fire him before the big race.

Working on a Burt Reynolds movie was almost like being on a family project. Burt surrounded himself with friends and that made for a very happy set. By this time Burt was married to Loni Anderson, and he told me that he especially wanted to hire me as a surprise for her. Loni and I had appeared in a TV movie called *Three on a Date* and got along great, so Burt felt I would fit right in with the cast he was assembling. The film was directed by Hal Needham, a former stuntman and one-time roommate of Burt's, and one of the screenwriters was Hugh Wilson, creator of the TV sitcom *WKRP in Cincinnati*, in which Loni had been a star. The cast included Burt's pals Ned Beatty and Jim Nabors, so pretty much everyone was comfortable with everyone else. When you're on location miles away from your home and family it really helps if you're surrounded by people you like. It was a pretty happy shoot.

One day Burt arranged for a little excursion for us. *Stroker Ace* was being shot not too far from the location of one of Burt's most memorable dramatic films, *Deliverance*. In that film Burt, Ned Beatty, Jon Voight, and Ronny Cox went down the Chattanooga River in Georgia in rubber rafts, and Ned's character had a really unpleasant encounter with one of the locals. Since we had a day off from shooting *Stroker Ace*, Burt rented rafts for the cast and crew and off we went on a white-water rafting adventure. When we got to the spot where they shot Ned's hillbilly encounter in the film, we beached the rafts and got out to take a look. Ned was prompted to do the pig squeal he did in the film, and being the good sport that he is, he did it with enthusiasm. In fact, there was so much enthusiasm that he did it several times and we all joined in squealing with him.

Something happened in the film that bothered me at first but made perfect sense later. There was a scene in which Burt, Jim Nabors, Parker Stevenson, and I were sitting at a picnic table. Stroker and Doc had not seen each other for a while, so Stroker asked me what I'd been doing over the years. I told him that I wanted to be a singer, but I couldn't succeed because I sounded too much like another singer who was already famous. When asked to give an example I sang the first few bars of Johnny Mathis's hit "It's Not for Me to Say" in an exaggerated version of Johnny's very distinctive style. It was completely unexpected, which made it pretty funny. However, I was a little disappointed that I was being asked to do an impression. I'd been hired to be an actor, not perform my club and TV routines. When I saw the completed film, the whole thing suddenly made sense. In the next scene Burt and Loni were dancing in a darkened bedroom suite to the song "It's Not for Me to Say." Not only was my Mathis impression unexpected and funny, but it was a perfect segue into the next scene.

As on most films, many of the *Stroker* locations were miles apart. The film transportation department arranged for vehicles and drivers to get everywhere they needed to go, but Burt and Loni always invited me to ride with them in their motor home. There was a bedroom in the back where they could have some privacy and relax, and I spent most of these moves talking with the driver, but Burt would pop out every once in a while for some conversation, and frequently he had a funny story to tell about something that had happened in his life or career. One of his stories that stands out in my mind was when he was working on *The Best Little Whorehouse in Texas* with Dolly Parton. He came up to Dolly and said, "If I take off my hairpiece and hug you between your breasts we'll look like the sign in front of a pawnshop." (If you're not old enough to remember when pawnshops had three dangling balls in front of them you might want to Google a picture. Burt was never too big to tell a joke on himself.)

A year or so later I was invited to take part in a tribute to Burt at a formal affair given by the Friars Club in the ballroom of the Century Plaza Hotel. Burt and Loni met me as I entered, and Burt put his right arm across my shoulders and proceeded to tell me what he wanted me to do in the way of impressions for him. As I said, Burt was a fan, so I was happy to take requests.

As we were waiting for the room to fill with friends and fans, I sat at the dais with Burt and Loni, Steve Allen, and several others who were to perform that night. Since I had to arrive early, my wife of a few years, Annie Gaybis, arrived alone just before the show and walked up to say hello to everybody before things got underway. Annie is an actress and dancer who keeps herself in good shape and it shows. Burt had never met her before. He turned to me and said, "Wow, where did you find her? I'll trade you!" There was an uncomfortable second and then Loni laughed. When she laughed we all had permission to laugh.

It wasn't the only uncomfortable moment that night. Later in the evening Burt went to the microphone to introduce his father, who was seated in the audience. Burt's dad was in his nineties and a retired sheriff from Jupiter, Florida. I'm sure he was very, very proud of Burt, but as he stood, Burt said, "He never said I love you to me." That was a little awkward.

The next time—and the last time—I saw Burt was a few years later in that same hotel ballroom. I had been asked by the Professional Dancers Society to perform at a tribute for two famous and beloved dancers, Bella Lewitzky and Ann Margret. I was in the lobby being interviewed when Burt arrived escorting Ann Margret. In all of the years I had worked in Las Vegas I had never met Ann, but Burt stopped and introduced us. We barely had time to exchange hellos when someone interrupted us and told me I had to get inside. At this event many of the performers were seated at tables in the audience, so I sat with my wife, Annie, and my piano accompanist, Rush Robinson, who was subbing for my regular pianist, Duane Smith, who was ill. We all enjoyed the show while I waited for my turn to perform.

Bella Lewitzky was the first to be honored that night, and a company of twenty or so dancers took the stage performing some of her choreography. Bella was known for her wild modern dance concepts, and the dancers appeared on stage as though they were birds released from their cage for the first time, jumping and soaring, waving and stretching to the music, and all making wonderful sense. It was crazy. I wasn't expecting that.

I turned to Rush and said, "Forget about the singers [I was going to impersonate], we may get to them later, but in the beginning play something wild." And that's what he did, piano wildness. I came out on stage like a clown being shot out of a cannon, bounding, cartwheeling, and doing just about any wild move I could imagine. When I ran out of gyrations I managed my way down stage to where Burt and Ann Margret were sitting, looked down, and said, "This is for you, Ann!" Then I put my hands on my hips shook my head and rested it on my right shoulder, which is her trademark move. The audience went wild. The whole thing was completely improvised and it was a huge hit. My dear departed friend, dancer-choreographer Miriam Nelson, was in the audience and exclaimed, "I loved it; it was wild abandon!"

I was feeling pretty good about the whole evening, especially after Burt and Ann complimented me on my performance. They then introduced me to another dancing legend, Gwen Verdon. Gwen told me she had wanted me for her costar in *Sweet Charity*, but they told her I was too young. I was actually twenty-eight when that show opened so . . . maybe they meant too young in the business. Who knows? And who are *they* anyway? *They* seem to get in the way a lot.

I loved Burt's final movie, *The Last Movie Star*. Try to see it if you haven't. In my experience, Burt Reynolds was a great guy. Yeah, he had problems and made his share of mistakes. We all do. But I cherish the memory of the big guy, the big smile and the big laugh, and the great times we spent together.

# Chapter Thirteen

### *Sitcomentaries*

$A$ s we go through life we sometimes get the opportunity to look at the same thing from different perspectives. Show business works that way, too. In the '90s I hosted a show called *Comedy on the Road*, which featured young comedians. On every episode, without fail, at least one of them would tell me that they watched me on television when they were a kid but never thought they would be working with me. I know how that goes. As a kid on Long Island, watching our beloved black-and-white Admiral television set, I never would've dreamed that I would ever get to meet, let alone work with, some of the people that I watched on that small screen. One of them was Danny Thomas.

Danny Thomas started as a nightclub comedian and radio actor, but by the time I was a teenager he was starting to appear in feature films. The big boost to his career, and the one that brought him into my living room once a week on the trusty Admiral, was a TV series entitled *Make Room for Daddy*. He played a nightclub entertainer named Danny Williams who struggled to be successful in his career while trying to be a good husband and father. The show was popular enough to last eleven years, and it allowed Danny to launch a new career as a television producer, where he was very successful. This success and visibility also gave Danny the platform to launch a non-showbiz project that was very important to him, the St. Jude Children's Hospital in Memphis, Tennessee. Danny and his wife toured the country raising money for several years and the hospital was opened in the early '60s. Today it's one of the premier research and treatment hospitals for children in the world. It's kind of hard not to like a guy who would do that.

Unlike many in Hollywood, Danny remained married to the same woman, Rose Marie Thomas, for decades, and two of their three children, Margaret (Marlo) and Tony, also went into the entertainment business. Marlo starred in a popular sitcom entitled *That Girl*, and Tony became a very successful television producer. In my career I ended up working with both Danny and Tony. All in all, the Thomas family left a pretty significant mark in the world of entertainment and medicine.

Speaking of medicine, in 1976 I worked on Danny Thomas's *The Practice*, a short-lived hospital sitcom. (How's that for a transition?) I played Dr. Roland Caine. Danny Thomas played Dr. Jules Bedford, an aging and slightly crotchety MD, and David Spielberg played Dr. David Bedford, his son. Shelley Fabares and the great character actress Dena Dietrich were also regulars, and the series drew some very heavy-hitter guest stars of the time such as Lucille Ball, Victor Buono, Bill Dana, David Huddleston, my friend Jayne Meadows, and Danny's daughter, Marlo Thomas. With a talent pool like that you would think the show would've had a long run, but unfortunately it only lasted twenty-seven episodes. I was happy and ready to do many more, but, that's the way it goes sometimes.

Like most sitcoms that are shot in front of a live audience, we rehearsed Monday through Thursday. The process began with the cast reading the script together for the first time on Monday, then we "put it on its feet" and rehearsed with the director. On Thursday they brought the cameras in to rehearse the shots, so by Friday we were ready to do the show. Actually, we did two shows on Friday. The first was considered a dress rehearsal. After that we all had dinner and listened to any final notes that the director, writers, and producers might have. Finally, we had our makeup touched up and wardrobe double-checked and we were ready to go.

Even though a sitcom is performed a lot like a play, it takes a certain amount of time to change scenes and reset cameras. The live audience and their response is important for the show in general, but as a performer, it's great to hear your lines get laughs. The one thing no one wants is for the audience to get bored while the show stops for technical adjustments. Usually a warm-up comic will perform before a show to get the audience in the mood to laugh, and also to step in during the downtime when the cameras are being reset. On *The Practice* we also had a musical trio that played as the audience entered and exited. The music was great for keeping the audience's energy up and giving the whole experience more of a special feel. Danny Thomas's wife, Mrs. Rose Marie Thomas, loved to get up there and sing with the trio. She was a professional singer and had a radio show in Detroit in 1936 when she met Danny, and she hadn't lost any of her talent.

There was a rumor that Danny liked to carry a lot of money on him. I have no idea if that was true or not, because I never asked him, but I did have an interesting experience with him once. On one of those late Friday nights Danny asked me to walk him to his car, which he parked on Pico Boulevard outside the gates of the 20th Century Fox studios. My first thought was, "Why in the world is Danny Thomas not parked on the lot?" Back before the studios built huge parking structures, getting a "drive-on" pass to park on the lot could sometimes be a problem, but that was for the people way down on the employment ladder. We're talking about Danny Thomas! He could park next to the stage—maybe even on the stage for all I know—but he definitely could park wherever he wanted to. Apparently, he wanted to park on the street, so off we went through the studio gate into the night.

As we walked and talked Danny was clutching an attaché case to his right side. About halfway to his car he turned to me and said, "Look at this." He then raised his arm to show me that along with the attaché case, he was holding a massive, long-barreled, single-shot pistol that he told me was chambered to take a .410 shotgun shell loaded with buckshot. I don't know what he had in that attaché case, but I sure didn't want to be the guy who tried to take it away from him.

Danny was a very personable guy who I enjoyed talking with whenever we had a chance. He was also a cigar smoker like many in the comedy business. George Burns, Milton Berle, Alan King . . . all cigar smokers. I guess I wasn't around the day the cigars were issued to comedians, but that's just fine with me. Anyway, Danny and I were talking one afternoon, and I noticed that when he put his cigar down the index finger on his cigar-holding hand remained curved down toward the thumb. In other words, the finger remained in the cigar-holding position even when the cigar was gone. I found that very curious. I started to notice it all the time with a kind of weird, obsessive interest. Finally, one day I couldn't stand it any longer. During a pause in the taping I asked what had happened to his finger. "I shot it off," he replied. I guess I would've been prepared for a lot of answers, but that wasn't one of them. I'm sure I must've said something, but I don't remember what. I decided to let that one go with no more questions.

As I mentioned, Danny Thomas's son, Tony, became a very successful producer with a long list of hits that included the television series *Benson*, *It's a Living*, *Beauty and the Beast*, and *The Golden Girls*. I was a semi-regular on the last two seasons of his sitcom *Soap*. I think this is where a misunderstanding occurred that has bothered me for a lot of years.

*Soap* had come and gone from the airwaves, and I hadn't seen Tony or his producing partner, Paul Junger Witt, for a long time. One afternoon in a supermarket parking lot in Malibu I ran into LeVar Burton, and I took a minute to help him load some food and drinks into his car for a party he was having. While we were doing this Paul drove by and shouted, "Hi, how you doing?" to LeVar. I shouted hello to him, but he didn't acknowledge me, so I trotted toward his truck. As I got closer he slowed down and I said, "How you doing?" when I got near his window. He didn't smile. "Is that all you got?" he replied and drove off. *What was that all about?* I wondered. It bothered me a little, but then anyone can have a bad day so I filed it in the back of my brain and let it go.

My encounter with Tony Thomas didn't happen until at least fifteen years later. I was at some tuxedo affair at the Bel Air Hotel, and at the conclusion of the evening when everyone was heading for the doors, I spotted Tony walking by holding the hand of a cute little boy. I called out, "Hey, Tony." He ignored me. I tried again, "Hey, Tony." He kept walking, ignoring me, until he got about ten yards away. Then he turned and said, "John, we heard what you said about us in the booth," and he turned his back and walked away. I had absolutely no idea what he was talking about. I put this together with the comment from Paul and it really bothered me, especially since I was completely clueless as to how I had offended them, and I certainly never would've done it on purpose. It took a while, but I finally figured out what must've happened.

It was the final show of the season, and there was a little wrap party with the cast and crew afterwards, not long, maybe a half hour. There was still a little work to do, but they didn't need the whole cast and crew, so only a few of us stayed late after the party. Billy Crystal and I both had some voiceover work. I was doing character voices; I don't remember what Billy was doing. The soundstage we were working on didn't have a real announcer's booth, so the crew had erected a tent-like structure with plastic windows. The tent would keep out the background noise while Billy and I sat on stools and read our lines into our microphones.

In this particular episode Richard Mulligan had to deal with space aliens. The space aliens were played by little people in head-to-toe costumes. I watched Richard and them through the window in the tent while I read my "alien lines" in a character voice at the appropriate moments. Billy did whatever he was supposed to do and then we took a break. Billy went to the control room to talk with the director and producers while I remained in the tent waiting to read again so we could finish the show and everyone could go home. No big deal.

While we were on this break and a whole lot of nothing was going on, the little people were stuck in the space alien costumes. I guess they got bored and started wrestling around with one another. In the navy we used to refer to that as "grab ass." If you're a bored eighteen-year-old in a naval barracks, it kind of comes with the territory, but it didn't seem appropriate to me on a professional soundstage. All I could think of was that if those guys tore their costumes we'd be there all night.

I never would've made a comment about it unless asked, and that's exactly what happened.

When Billy came back into the tent he said in a gangster-type voice, "Whatya tink o' dees guys?" Assuming he meant the two guys goofing off on stage, I replied, "They're morons." The microphones were open and our voices were being pumped into the control room. Tony and Paul couldn't see the grab-ass performance on stage, so they apparently thought I was talking about them. Either that, or Billy was referring to Tony and Paul and I was talking about the little people. Whichever way it went down, it was a misunderstanding that I wish I could've cleared up.

I'm not a big social guy and I'm certainly not a gossip. Rarely do I make negative comments about people, and when that happens there is always what I think is a good reason for it. If I don't have something good to say about someone, I generally say nothing at all. This misunderstanding was particularly upsetting because I had great admiration for the producers on *Soap*. I really enjoyed working with them and had great respect for the way Tony, Paul, and Susan Harris could watch a rehearsal that wasn't going quite right and make the sketch work just by changing a word or an entrance. All these years later I still feel bad about this episode.

Misunderstandings happen once in a while, but they aren't all terrible. In fact, looking back, a few were funny. There are times I think of and smile, things that happened by error or a response to a situation. Two of them stand out . . . I'll give you the long way around.

As a new guy in Hollywood, I had to learn some things the hard way. I suppose that's true in a lot of careers, but most people don't have to make their mistakes in front of an audience. Show folks have their list of "dos" and "definitely don't dos." Unfortunately, they don't hand the new guys a copy of the list when they enter the business, so we frequently have to learn the hard way. For example, there is applause. In the beginning of your career one receives applause after a performance, but when one begins to gain a bit of popularity the audience, if they like that person's work, will applaud as soon as that individual first appears on stage. That's fine in a nightclub, but it can be a bit awkward in other situations.

The first sitcom I was on was a "closed set"; there was no live studio audience and pretty much no one around who wasn't directly involved with the show. It was called *Accidental Family* and starred Jerry Van Dyke and Lois Nettleton. I played Jerry's friend from Las Vegas, and when it came time for me to enter in my first scene I did so naturally, without applause. I'd greet Jerry and Lois, then continue with my lines. No problem.

My next sitcom was a little different. I was cast to play a humane control officer—what people used to call a dog-catcher—in a sketch comedy pilot for television staring Eve Arden. If you're old enough you may remember Eve, who was wonderful as the wisecracking teacher in the '50s sitcom *Our Miss Brooks*. This particular show was a pilot—an initial, demonstration episode—so the network executives could see how people reacted to it and if they wanted to produce the series and put it in their broadcast lineup. The show had a live audience in the house, which is really great for comedy. It means a lot to a comedian to actually hear the audience laughing at your lines. Anyway, my character entered halfway through the program and I got a big round of applause from the studio audience as I stepped onto the stage. Naturally, coming from a background in nightclubs and variety TV shows, my first response was to acknowledge the audience by nodding and smiling to them. Everything *stopped.*

"Hold it, let's do Mr. Byner's entrance again," someone yelled. *Oh yeah,* I remembered, *there's not supposed to be a bunch of people applauding when someone walks into Eve Arden's home.* Lesson learned.

The other experience that stands out involved the man who had been the producer of *Accidental Family* a few years earlier, Mr. Sheldon Leonard. Sheldon had been a character actor playing mostly tough-guy parts and had a gruff voice that he could make menacing or hilarious depending on the role. In the movie *Guys and Dolls* Sheldon played Harry the Horse, which was pretty much the way he was in real life. In the '50s he left acting to become a television producer and director and had incredible success. Sheldon was producing this pilot, which starred another character actor, Henry Jones.

Henry was one of those guys who you see on the screen and immediately recognize. You may not remember what you saw him in at first, but when you think about it you realize you have seen him in just about *everything.* Henry had an incredible long and successful career in TV and films. Co-starring were Michele Lee and the multitalented comedian Ruth Buzzi. The plot went like this: Henry Jones runs a greeting card store and hires Ruth and Michele to write the clever sayings, poems, whatever, for the cards. I was a guest star on the pilot cast to play a thief that Ruth and Michele discover in their shared apartment. Great cast, great part, great producer . . . I was looking forward to having a good time.

On the first morning of the reading of the script, everyone was gathered at the long table in the studio where the show would be taped. This would be the first of many, many, many times we would perform this over the course of the week. All of the important people were huddled around taking notes, and the writers were especially keen on hearing their words out loud for the first time to see if they were really as funny as they thought they were. At the head of the table sat Sheldon, like a king over his court.

We opened the script and each of us began to read our assigned lines aloud for the first time. As they spoke their lines, the rest of the cast did so with gusto. They dove right into some kind of performance. When it came to me I just read the lines as you might read aloud a sentence or two to somebody from a newspaper . . . with little to no emotion . . . just reading my part. I wasn't being lazy. It was something very basic. I had to know the situation my character was in and how he related to the story that was taking place. After all, we were going to be working on this for a week.

Well, when the last page was read and the script was finally closed, there was an uncomfortable silence around the table as the rest of the cast and writers tried to figure out how I'd gotten the job. Finally, Sheldon broke the silence with his tough-guy, Brooklyn accent. "Don't worry. Byner's a slow starter!" Thank you, Sheldon Leonard! By the way, the pilot went off without one hitch. I love memories. Especially the ones that make me smile.

In 1990, as I mentioned earlier, I was invited to host a traveling TV show called *Comedy on the Road*. The idea was to travel this country and a few other countries and book local stand-up comedians and shoot a show in their own hometown. We had to have a title sequence for the show made, and the producers asked me if I had any ideas. I suggested that it would be fun to have me driving down a winding road with the names of the acts to be on that show printed on billboards as I passed them. Everybody loved the idea and the guy in charge of making the title sequence did an outstanding job. He shot me sitting on a green stool with my feet on a green box holding a car steering wheel. He then made a fantasy cartoon cityscape world with bits of random art and photographs with all kinds of fun stuff in it. He even had me driving through a car wash. When he matted everything together in the green screen process, it was me driving an invisible car (The Nothingmobile) through a fantasy neighborhood. It was colorful and funny and set the tone for the whole show.

Like most shows the performers had to audition to get booked, but since many of them were not in Los Angeles they sent in videotapes of their nightclub performances. We really had no idea how many comics were in the country until the mail carrier started dumping bags of tape at the office. Many of them were called and told they couldn't use some of the language they had on their tape if hired. *Comedy on the Road* was on the A&E network, and they had a pretty strict standards and practices policies at the time. They wanted a family-friendly show and as I'm sure you know, comedy club acts are frequently anything but family friendly. We told them their act would be riddled with bleeps if, on the show, they couldn't talk without those adjectives, pronouns, or whatever the effing things are. Well, they agreed, of course, because they wanted to be on TV but, lo and behold, some of them actually could not manage to get through their seven-minute set without dropping the F-bomb or something else. Don't ask.

We traveled to many cities, met many people, and had many good times, except for once when I was walking out of a theater in one of the cities with my friend, Doug Wellman, who was the producer of *Comedy on the Road*. It had been about a half hour since we'd finished taping the show—I'd had enough time to get out of my makeup—when we ran into a guy standing alone in the otherwise empty theater lobby. He called my name and had a big, excited smile on his face. He said he was a fan, walked over to us, and we chatted for a few minutes until I pointed out that we had a car waiting for us. I said we had to get going, and he asked if he could give me a hug. I said sure. (Some people want an autograph, some people want a handshake, a few want a hug. I draw the line at tongue kissing.)

The next thing I knew the guy had me in a choke hold. He said, "You know I could break your neck right now?" I looked at Doug, who stared back at me with a look of shock mixed with wonder as he considered what other host he could book to finish the season if the guy killed me. It only lasted for a few seconds but felt a whooole lot longer. When he released me he said, "I'm just kidding!" Very (not) funny. Ah, the things you remember.

Doug Wellman is a pretty funny guy in his own right. We spent a lot of time traveling around the country together. We became pretty close and remain that way. Doug had a date with a comedienne one night and the next day I asked him how it went. "Well," he said, "she was wearing leather, denim, lace, sequins, rivets, and diamonds. I felt like I was having dinner with a trout lure."

Another time we were flying out of Chicago in a storm. Something had happened—we had to get our tickets at the last minute or something—and we were sitting in the middle of the plane. As we took off, the plane started bouncing like you wouldn't believe. We both looked at the cabin attendant, who appeared terrified, her eyes the size of dinner plates. That's never a good sign. Doug and I looked at one another and he said to me, "Oh, John, I can't believe we're going to die sitting in coach."

After our clever animated title sequence I would say, "From (city name), it's *Comedy on The Road* and here's me." I always opened the show with a monologue, like the late-night shows do, before introducing the first guest comic. Well, there were comedy writers for the show who did a good job, but sometimes the material I was given would poke fun at things about the city we were in. Some audiences would find that funny, but some wouldn't. We stopped making comments about the cities. Also, every comic has their style and not all jokes are equally funny coming from different comics. To make the material more personal, my brother Tom and I would add to the scripts. Tom had a history of writing for several sitcoms, and a few comedy albums, so it wasn't nepotism in this case. He had good credits. And he knew me and my style. In fact, I would say he knew me like a brother, but he *is* my brother . . . so I guess I can leave that out.

We traveled all over the United States as well as Mexico, Canada, and England. The show aired for four seasons and some of our guest comics who were just starting out back then went on to have their own shows. I admire stand-up comics that work the comedy club circuits these days, mostly for their stick-to-it attitude. Life on the road is tough. When I began in the early '60s, there weren't a lot of comics in the business. At one time I actually read that the great comedian Red Skelton figured there were about a hundred professional comedians in the world. Today there are probably more than that many in each state. There weren't any comedy clubs of any kind when I was starting out. We worked in clubs that headlined singers, musicians, and in one case, I opened for Blackstone the Magician. In most comedy clubs these days there aren't dressing rooms; it's the boss's office, one's car, or you just have to hang out at the bar. In some comedy clubs, especially in big cities, there's a green room, filled with comics, their friends or family members, and the guy who won't stop talking, usually about himself. As I said, life on the road is tough.

As we did *Comedy on the Road*, particularly when we were in some of the smaller cities, I would look at some of the young comics getting their first break and remember how I started. At the first club I worked in, The Oaks in Syosset, Long Island, at least between shows, the house trio and I were allowed to hang out in the kitchen. Later, the hotel casinos I worked had dressing rooms fit for a human with a telephone, sofa, restroom, coffee maker, TV, and yes, even room service. It kind of spoiled me. I don't think I would want to have to go back to getting dressed in a leaky restroom.

Over the four years of *Comedy on the Road* I met a lot of people, made some new friends, and had some great meals. And here's a sweet tale of travel and kindness. Doug and I flew first class, but the rest of the crew flew coach. After one of our shows, I think it was in Chicago, one of the production staff, Ron Kantor, and I were sitting together in the waiting area for our flight back to Los Angeles. Ron was a terrific guy with a wonderful sense of humor, so we were having a pretty good time reflecting on the show we'd just done and watching the travelers pass back and forth in front of us. Ron was holding his coach ticket, and I was holding my first-class ticket. A guy in an orange jumpsuit walked past us and recognized me. A little while later he returned, stopped in front of us, and asked if Ron was with me. I said yes, and the guy turned to Ron and said, "You're going first class too. There'll be a ticket for you at the gate." No name, just a guy in an orange jumpsuit with clout saying have a good flight as he continued on. God bless him, wherever he is.

And on behalf of the road warrior comics traveling everywhere, if you go to a comedy club with your friends, 'cause that's usually how it goes, please don't try to be funnier than the act. Remember, your friends and everyone else in the room came to see and hear the person on stage. If that person doesn't do well by your standards, hold on, there'll be another comic who may think like you. At that very moment he or she may be getting dressed in a leaky restroom just to make you happy.

# Chapter Fourteen

### *Hi-Yo, Silver Screen*

On a movie or TV shooting set the assistant directors pretty much run everything. The first assistant director is in charge of making sure everything and everyone is in the right place and things are moving quickly and efficiently. If you're hearing someone speaking loudly and giving orders on a film set, it's probably the 1st AD. Like most other industries, film has its own special language spoken by the insiders. For example, you don't turn off a motion picture light, you "kill" it. There is a particular type of small motion-picture light known as a baby. So, if you're standing on a soundstage and somebody yells, "Kill the baby!" you might want to investigate before you call the police. Having been on several television sitcoms, I was used to the lingo used by the assistant directors, like "That's lunch," "Back at two" (from lunch), "Hold the talking," "That's fifteen" (minute break), and of course, "That's a wrap," which generally means we've completed the show and it's over.

In 1971, a friend named Susan brought me up to the offices of a production company to meet a director named Peter Bogdanovich, to talk to him about a part in a movie he was going to direct called *What's Up, Doc?* You almost never know if you've got the job when you leave an audition, so there is usually a bit of anxious waiting involved if it's a job you really want. Fortunately, I received a call a few days later and was told to check in with Western Costume for a tuxedo they had waiting for me, and then head over to Warner Bros. Studios in Burbank. I would have considered this picture a major feather in my cap—if I wore caps—because this was really an "A" picture with an all-star cast. First of all, Peter Bogdanovich was a hot young director at the time. His previous film, *The Last Picture Show*, had gotten a ton of critical acclaim and boosted him up the Hollywood ladder to the point where he could get the great scripts and the great stars. He got both on this one. The script was by Buck Henry and the stars were Barbra Streisand and Ryan O'Neal. Streisand, in addition to a vibrant recording career, had just starred in *Hello, Dolly!* O'Neal had just had a huge hit with *Love Story*. For a guy who hadn't been in the business all that long, and who had never been in a movie, I was hanging out with some very big people.

On the first day I was supposed to shoot, I arrived at the Warner Bros. lot, got into my tux, went to makeup, and headed to the stage at the appointed hour. I sat, waiting to be told what to do, and passed the time talking to some of the extras. They never called me for my scene. I took off the tuxedo and makeup and headed home. On the second day I arrived at Warner Bros., got into my tux, went to makeup, and headed to the stage at the appointed hour. I watched them shoot some bits and pieces, but they never called me for my scene. I took off the tuxedo and makeup and headed home. On the third day—you know the drill by now—I was on the stage at the appointed hour, but this time Peter Bogdanovich came over to have a word with me. He told me to hang on. The sequence that I was going to be in wasn't scripted, but they would soon have something for me. He also told me I was to play a musicologist. Ah . . . okay.

On the fourth day or so, I was running out of stories and bits to do for the extras when I casually looked at my tux jacket lining and discovered it had originally been worn by Bing Crosby. His name was printed just above the inside pocket, and just as I was thinking *WOW*, Peter said that I was in the next scene. Double WOW!

The scene took place at a round table, and I took my seat among a few guys and Barbra Streisand. While waiting for the crew to finish the camera set-up, one of the guys sitting next to me said to Barbra, "John does an impression of George Jessel." Barbra, of course, said, "Let's hear it!" I said a few words, and she broke up laughing as Ryan O'Neal entered the set. Barbra said to him, "Ryan, John impersonates George Jessel!" Ryan said, "WHY!!?" That made *me* break up. I thought it was a great question and didn't have an answer.

Shortly after, we were given our lines and told to say them as we ducked under the table from our seated position. We rehearsed this once and it became pretty clear that it wasn't going to work. Tables are made to have things on top of them, not people under them. The table would have to be raised some to accommodate all of us under it. The crew stepped in, made the proper adjustments, and we were ready again. When the takes were completed, the assistant director entered and yelled for all to hear, "That's a wrap!" As far as I knew, that was fini, the end, no more, it's over. I said my goodbyes, turned in my tux, and went home where I gathered my kids and proceeded to Antigua in the British Virgin Islands. I had leased a place across from Admiral Nelson's Dock Yard, a beautiful spot to take the family for a vacation in a tropical paradise.

A day or so later, at three in the morning, my phone rang. It was my manager telling me that the production company was waiting for me in San Francisco. We had only wrapped for the location, not the whole movie. Oops. It was too late to get to San Francisco then, so my first movie consisted of one line. Whenever I see Ryan, we talk about that line and smile. From then on I've always had scripts to check on so I know what's happening, regardless of what the assistant director yells.

One of the great things about being in the comedy business is that you get to work with some funny, creative people, and sometimes the work itself is pretty far out. It's not like going to an office every day. In 1985, Rudy De Luca, one of the writers of my 1972 *John Byner Comedy Hour* show and a friend ever since, called me and said he'd like to have me in a movie that he he'd written and planned to direct. Rudy is a frequent collaborator of Mel Brooks, and he has an amazing ability to take any situation and shape it into something strangely hilarious. I knew this film was going to be special when he told me the title, *Transylvania 6-5000*. (If you have a few years on you, you'll recognize the title as a riff on the Glenn Miller hit, "Pennsylvania 6-5000.")

I really wanted to do the film, especially when Rudy told me the great people who already signed for the cast. The only problem was my schedule. I was on a break from the *Bizarre* series, but I had bookings at various clubs and casinos, and it took a bit of work to sort all of that out. I was going to need to clear a significant amount of time. You see, we would be shooting on location in Zagreb, Yugoslavia, which is now Croatia. This wasn't the kind of deal where I could film all week and then hop a plane to do a weekend gig at the Vegas Hilton. Once you're in Zagreb you're pretty much there for the long haul. The location was very important for this film because we needed a real castle. Not a lot of those here in the States.

*Transylvania 6-5000* was a "Fronkenshteen" monster movie, as the Zagreb actors pronounced it, but it also featured mummies, werewolves, and a nymphomaniac vampire, played by Geena Davis. Rudy put in a little something for everyone. The cast was outstanding. I played Radu, a hunched-over servant who worked for the mayor, and Carol Kane played my wife, Lupi. We had a ball working with Jeff Goldblum, Joseph Bologna, Ed Begley Jr., Michael Richards, Norman Fell, and Teresa Ganzel, along with many talented local actors and extras.

Circumstances allowed the cast to get to know one another in a slightly different way than on other pictures. The castle was about forty miles outside of Zagreb, and in the early spring that big stone hulk was "colder than a brass toilet seat," as they say. The place was probably comfortable by the end the summer, but that didn't help us at the time. While the crew changed set ups and relit, we all fled to the relative comfort of a large trailer that had been provided for us. Rather than all going off to different dressing rooms, we actually got to sit around and become friends. Carol Kane was a delight and I got to know her very well. In fact, Carol told me about her mother, who at the time sang and played piano in a fancy nightery in Paris, and invited me to go there with her when the picture wrapped. I would've loved to have gone, but I had to return to my pre-arranged dates in the US of A. I loved working with Carol; we had fun.

There was also a really unusual life coincidence on this picture. I met Ed Begley Jr. for the first time, but for years I'd been getting postcards from his dad. Here's how his famous actor father and I connected. I was nine years old, living in North Merrick, Long Island, and going to public school. My parents would have enrolled me in the Catholic school, but we moved from Laurelton in the middle of the school year and the Catholic school in Merrick was all filled up. To make sure my spiritual education wasn't neglected I was sent to religion (or catechism) classes once a week, and was invited to join the choir.

One day the nun in charge of the choir announced that a man named Ed Begley—"a famous actor," although I'm not sure I understood that at the time—was going to take the entire choir to see the Dodgers play in Brooklyn. On that day I got the "okay to go" slip signed by my dad, who told me that Ed Begley was the voice of The Fat Man on the radio, so that put things in perspective. My dad always listened to ball games on the radio, so I told him to listen for my whistle. I recall we choir members rode in a wood-paneled station wagon, while Mr. Begley, being driven in a sedan, came up alongside us now and then to wave. In the stadium that day, I whistled my head off, and it seemed the entire crowd was whistling . . . such competition! When I returned home I asked my father if he had heard my whistle, and like a good guy, he said yes.

Fast forward to twenty-one years later, I'm in show biz in Hollywood and a friend had to drop off a script at Ed Begley's home, so I went along for the ride. I couldn't wait to finally thank him for that ball game in 1947. He remembered the day, and for a few years after he'd send me a postcard once every few months from a place on the road where he was doing a play or working on a film. He called me once to announce that his teenaged son wanted to be a comedian and asked if I had any advice for him. I told him what I usually tell people who want to know for a relative or themselves: try to keep close to the vest, talk about things you know about and have noticed or experienced, and to be one's self. Not that any of this applied, but a few years later, Ed Begley Jr. and I were in a movie together. Who knew?

Most actors have a process they go through for getting into

character before a scene. There are different types of training such as method acting, and on the other side of the scale there are some who have little quirks that resemble superstition. Becoming another person and being true to all of that character's personality traits is harder than it seems. Before I go into a scene, I like to imagine my character's physical characteristics, like his posture. Getting rid of tension is also important.

I noticed that Jeff Goldblum had a process he went through before a scene. I'd see him standing behind a door he was to enter, or behind a wall he was to walk around, and he'd prepare for his entry by jumping up and down, shaking himself, and then straightening his clothes in time for "Action!" Michael Richards astounded me with his physical abilities. Several times he was called on to fall flat on his back on a concrete floor. He did it every time without having to be rushed off in an ambulance, which I thought was pretty impressive.

Joseph Bologna was a quiet guy, but he loved to laugh. He turned in some great comedic performances in films over the years, but his approach to acting was very serious. There was a place in the film where Joseph had to switch characters in mid-scene. He changed from the calm Dr. Malavaqua to the mad scientist just by walking through the door into his laboratory. Basically, he had to play two different characters in the same scene and make the change while he was walking. He was having a problem making the change and asked me to assist him. I guess he figured that since I changed characters so abruptly in my act I might have some useful advice. I was happy to show him how to do the physical stuff and did the scene a few times for him. He got it immediately and did the scene perfectly when the camera rolled.

Unfortunately, later on in the shoot I pissed him off. It was a scene in the village square. It was night and it was really cold. Local extras in costumes had circled the square holding lit torches. Some kind of stuff from the torches was dripping down their arms. Geena Davis was in a horse-drawn, open carriage, wearing a seductive, and tiny, vampire costume that exposed too much of her to the elements. You could see everybody's breath. Everyone was standing there freezing while we waited for Joe to do some lines. Joe apparently had some questions about his motivation for the scene, and he was talking to director Rudy. The whole thing was taking what seemed to be forever.

I was freezing and couldn't stand it any longer. In frustration I broke the cold, smoky silence by yelling, "Let's goooo!" Not very professional, but successful. The scene was shot, the wagon took off, someone threw a coat on Geena, and the crowd dispersed when "Cut, that's a print" was announced. I was looking forward to getting anyplace warm, but Joe followed me out of the town square, saying all the way, "Is that how you act when you're doing your *Bizarre* show?" and things of that nature. After warming up, I called his room to apologize. He understood and we remained friends.

Rudy would release cast members as they finished their scenes, so not everyone was dismissed from the set at the same time. When a group of us had finished our scenes for the day, a van was standing by to take us back to the hotel while the rest of the cast and crew continued with other scenes. I noticed while riding with Geena Davis that she liked to softly sing to herself as she looked out at the scenery going by as we rode back to the hotel. On one trip, I recognized a tune she was singing and began to harmonize with her. Her face lit up as though I had found her favorite pet, and we sang a bit louder the rest of the way. I knew how she felt. While in the service, I often asked someone who could sing if I could harmonize with them. Having sung like that with my family while growing up, I missed doing it when away from home. If the person I asked agreed, most of the time they would inadvertently slip up to the harmony line, and that would be the end of that. But I must say, Geena and I sounded great together. She is a treasure, as nice as she is beautiful.

When the location days came to a close Rudy was happy, we all had fun, and all these years later *Transylvania 6-5000* still shows up on television at Halloween.

# Chapter Fifteen

## *The Great White Way*

In the spring of 2004, the unpredictable winds of show business blew something my way that I hadn't thought about since 1958. That's a fair amount of time between thoughts, and I'll start at the beginning, way back when.

In 1958 I was fresh out of the service and trying to figure out what to do with my life. I enjoyed performing for my family, friends, and shipmates, but I wasn't even dreaming of making a life of show business. A friend of the family, Joe Calcagno, whom I mentioned earlier, had an in with someone who was auditioning red-headed guys who could sing for a new Broadway show called *Kelly*. I had red hair and I could sing, so Joe figured I at least had the minimum qualifications for the gig. Joe's son, Dean, played piano, so Joe got us together and had us rehearse a few songs that we could present at the audition. He suggested we cover our bases by rehearsing one slow song and one with a quick tempo. For the slow one we chose "Sentimental Journey" and "Almost Like Being in Love" for the up-tempo option. In the Calcagno house there was a very large, beautiful grand piano with a very rich, full sound. As it turned out, sound would be the key element in this story, although not exactly as we anticipated.

Dean and I rehearsed and had things down pretty well, so when it came time to take the train into Manhattan from Rockville Centre where we lived, we were ready—or so we thought. When we arrived backstage at the Broadhurst

Theater there were more red-headed guys than I had ever seen anywhere, ever, at one time. Seriously, take a look around you now. How many red-headed people do you see? We're usually a small minority, but backstage in that theater there had to be close to two dozen red-haired guys, all about my age. It was actually kind of . . . weird.

Dean and I took a seat in the flock of redheads and waited for my name to be called. It wasn't too long before we were walking from the dim wings onto the huge, empty stage and into the bright lights. They don't give you much to work with at an audition. The stagehands in the theaters are all in the union and they get paid pretty good money. Since it's an audition and there is no paying audience, the producers keep costs down by providing as few things as possible in order to minimize the number of stagehands they have to hire. You get just enough lights for them to see you, and a microphone so they can hear you. Other than that, you're standing alone on an empty Broadway stage the size of a parking lot. To make the experience even more intimidating, you're looking out into empty seats, maybe 1,500 or 1,600 of them. The whole thing is eerie.

Dean and I stepped onto the stage of that big, old, beautiful theater and shielded our eyes from the bright stage lights for a moment while they adjusted from the dim backstage area. I could see the microphone on a stand and what appeared to be a small piano. We'd been told that we were only going to be allowed to perform one tune, so we chose the up-tempo "Almost Like Being in Love." I walked to the mic as Dean took his place at the keyboard. I looked out at the near-empty theater and finally spotted four gentlemen, rather older, seated together in the center section, about a third of the way up the aisle. They had little lights shining on their faces attached to the backs of the seats in front of them, which were the quality of dim flashlights. They didn't identify themselves; they were just four sets of eyes, noses, and lips. I suppose they were the director, playwright, and a couple of producers, but they were keeping it a secret as far as we were concerned.

Shortly one of them said, "Go ahead." I took a breath, Dean began to play the first few bars of the introduction . . . and it ended right there. The keyboard instrument turned out to be a clavinet. Compared to the Calcagno piano we'd rehearsed with, the thing sounded like something you could buy for five dollars in a toy store. Seriously, that's exactly what it sounded like, a child's toy piano. Imagine Schroeder in the *Peanuts* comic strip. The whole thing caught us completely off guard. Here we were at the center of the American theater and the piano sounded like something you would give to a four-year-old. I began to laugh. I couldn't help it and I had no way to stop it, it just popped out. Dean stopped playing and as I turned to him he broke up laughing too. The whole thing was absurd. I struggled to regain control, apologized, and we started again. Too late. It was like when you were told by your parents you couldn't laugh at a certain time, and when you tried to muffle it you made it worse. We gave it one more shot, but after trying three times it was "Thank you!" from one of the lighted faces, and that concluded my first fling with Broadway. Dean and I laughed all the way back home.

As I mentioned earlier in this book, Dean and his dad were great friends who were very kind and helpful to me when I was starting out. You'll recall it was Dean who accompanied me at the Oaks Club, in Syosset, Long Island in the very early start of my career, and on Merv Griffin's *Talent Scouts* show in 1963. Dean and I are still in touch, still pals, and still laughing. That friendship has lasted a lifetime. Anyway, the show, *Kelly*, opened on February 6, 1965, and closed on February 6, 1965, a glorious one-night run that cost the investors $650,000. The rumor was that the next day the sets were burned in a dump in New Jersey. I have many times thanked God I didn't get that job. I survived without Broadway and Broadway survived without me, although I did wonder a few times over the years what it would be like to experience performing on the Great White Way. As it turned out, I would get another chance.

My wife, Annie, and I like to travel by train. It's relaxing and there's a whole lot more to look at in this country while traveling that way than over the tops of clouds. Before Hurricane Katrina wiped out a lot of train tracks that haven't been replaced yet, Annie and I did the Florida to Los Angeles trip by train once a year for several years. Annie is a member of the SHARE (Share Happily and Reap Endlessly) Organization. All of the members are ladies who rehearse song and dance numbers for six weeks to perform a one-night-only charity show at the Hilton Hotel in Beverly Hills. The money they raise goes to support needy children, and they have been doing this successfully for many years. The show was the idea of Jeanne Martin, Dean Martin's first wife, and Annie looks forward to participating every year. I look forward to watching.

In 2004 we were on the train, about halfway back to Florida, when there came a call from my agent, telling me I had to get to New York as soon as possible. I told her we were on the train in the middle of nowhere and it would have to wait until we got back to our home in Jacksonville, Florida. A day or so later, I flew, which I rarely do, to New York's Kennedy Airport where a waiting limo drove me to a very nice hotel not far from Lincoln Center. There I was to audition for Nathan Lane and Susan Stroman, two people I'd never met. They were putting up a new show called *The Frogs* with Nathan as the star and Susan as the director/choreographer, and there was a role in it they thought I would be right for. That sounded good to me, so off I went to the meeting.

The meeting was all very nice and friendly and after talking to them for a bit they asked to hear my singing voice. I hadn't overanalyzed the audition process, I just picked out a song that I like to sing. Without realizing it I chose a song that Nathan had sung hundreds, maybe thousands, of times before when he appeared on Broadway in *Guys and Dolls*. When auditioning it's usually best to pick something a bit different, so when I told the audition pianist I was going to sing "Luck Be a Lady" he looked at me in astonishment and said, "Are you kidding?" I wasn't expecting that. I told him I wasn't kidding and off we went.

When I finished they said that it was fine, and the whole thing was pleasant and painless. Nathan asked if I was staying the night, and if so would I like to catch the show he was then starring in, *The Producers*. Yes, of course I would. Extremely funny show. Nathan and company were outstanding. I have to say the best part was after the show when I went backstage to thank Nathan and to compliment him. It was there he told me that I had the part. I gave him a hug, returned to my hotel, where on my voicemail I heard Susan Stroman's voice saying, "Welcome to Broadway." It took forty-six years, but I was back.

I went home elated and a week or so later, Annie and I packed up our bikes, enough clothes and things for a couple of seasons (we don't have a lot of overcoat weather in Jacksonville—we're pretty much one-season people now), and headed up to New York, where we checked in to our newly provided digs, a lovely apartment on the thirtieth floor of

Number One, West 64th Street, overlooking Tavern On The Green in Central Park. As they say in real estate, it's location, location, location, and our location couldn't have been better. We were right across the street from Lincoln Center where the rehearsals and show were to take place for a total of twenty weeks, six weeks rehearsing and fourteen weeks of scheduled performances. A three-minute commute—hard to find these days.

The show was a fine experience about an unusual subject. It was all about hell. I played two brothers. (Not at the same time, of course—I'm not quite that versatile.) My entrance in the show was far from usual. At a certain point Nathan Lane's character, accompanied by his assistant, played by Roger Bart, called out, "Boatman, boatman, where's the boatman?" and the orchestra played the intro to the song "All Aboard," music and lyrics by Stephen Sondheim. With that, I descended from the rigging thirty-five feet above the stage, standing in a skiff and singing the song. I was decked out in a long white wig, mustache, and beard, wearing a heavy, brown, monk-style robe.

What I was *not* wearing for the first few shows was a safety belt, but then someone thought the possibility of an actor tumbling thirty-five feet onto the boards might be an unwanted distraction, so about six shows into the run they secured me to the rigging. A couple of times the skiff got a bit shaky, but for the most part I felt safe. This added another interesting element to my performance. In addition to thinking about singing and acting I now had to deal with this contraption. About twenty minutes into the show a wardrobe assistant would arrive at my dressing room door holding the belt. It contained hooks that were attached to the rigging, which was secured to the latches on the skiff. He and I would walk up the four or five flights of steps to the stage rafters where we'd sit on a bench until we'd get a cue from a stagehand. He would then lock my belt latches on to the rigging and we'd listen for Nathan's "Where is the boatman?" music to begin. On that cue the boat would descend to the stage as I sang this happy (not!) ditty:

All aboard Haiti's Express,
non stop, just a short hop
to the bottomless pit,
this is it, Club Dead
Straight ahead.
Bring your shroud
no Coffins allowed
there's too big a crowd
But if you're a stiff
then get in the skiff
and we're off to Perdition

And wait till you see perdition . . . it goes on, but you'll have to buy the CD. It's really good. Near the end of the song I'd disconnect myself from the rigging so the stagehands could haul it back up, leaving me and the boat on the stage. I'd meet Nathan and Roger at the dock, welcome them aboard, and we'd begin our trip down the River Styx. Great show, great cast, great fun.

An aside to let you know that Nathan Lane is a golden character. He refers to himself as Mr. Broadway, and he's not exaggerating. One of the interesting facts of life is that inconvenient things don't stop happening to you just because you're in a Broadway show. Life—the good and the bad—goes on. One morning I woke up and realized a lower front tooth had chipped off at the gum line during the night. This isn't a big deal if you work as a telemarketer in the basement of a tenement somewhere, but it's really not good news when you're performing and singing in front of a live audience on Broadway. I didn't have a chance to have it looked at by a dentist or let my fellow actors know, so during the matinee that afternoon I tried to hide the gap by doing my lines with my lower lip kind of up over my lower teeth. I figured the mustache and beard would hide it.

Oh, I hid the missing tooth all right, but I created another problem. After that first show Roger Bart called my dressing room to tell me that Nathan was wondering what might be causing me to talk like that. It seems that in covering up my missing tooth I'd created a speech impediment. I showed Roger the problem and he went back to explain to Nathan. Someone set me up with a dental appointment for the next day and I forgot about the whole thing to the degree possible. However, Nathan didn't forget. During the performance that night when we were halfway around our trip standing in the skiff, Nathan said to me, "Let me see where you lost your tooth. Hold it everybody!" and everything stopped, actors, orchestra, everything. "Show the audience the empty space between your teeth," he projected in his best Broadway voice. I did as requested. Then he said to all, "Okay, we continue," and off we went. The next day I had a temporary tooth inserted, and I've always been able to claim I gave a show-stopping performance on Broadway.

Now I know what it's like to be on Broadway, the Great White Way, New York City. I met new friends, sang new music, and had new experiences. What could be better? Thank you, Susan Stroman, Nathan Lane, and his supportive brothers;

they're big fans of mine. Nathan, you're the best. And if my agent is reading this . . . you are, too.

# Chapter Sixteen

### *Evenings to Remember to Forget*

S ince I'm not a real big social person, I never made it a point to hit all the big Hollywood parties or to be seen in the top nightclubs and restaurants, but I really do like people. All kinds of people. Some of them may be celebrities, and others are just people I like to play a round of golf with or talk to while sitting on the patio looking at the boats in the marina. I don't pick my friends by their social status. As a performer I've accumulated a pretty large group of fans over the years and I enjoyed meeting them. Ninety-nine percent of them are terrific. However, the 1 percent—bless their hearts—can be a little challenging.

In my career, particularly at the beginning, I had to do an awful lot of traveling. Television appearances are usually limited to Los Angeles and New York, and the casino show rooms were primarily in Las Vegas, Reno, and Atlantic City. When you perform regularly in cities like that you pick up a few friends so you never really have to be alone, but in the early days, when I was working club dates in various cities, I could get pretty tired of sitting alone in a hotel room. Sometimes fans will come to your rescue. You will meet them at the place you're performing, have a conversation, and sometimes things just click and you enjoy being with them. Many times in these situations the people invited me to come over for a home-cooked meal. The majority of these were great fun, but a few were horrific.

Years ago I was working a small club outside of Cleveland, Ohio, and after the second show the club owner knocked on my dressing room door and told me that there was a group of fans that had remained at their table in the hopes that I would join them for a drink. He told me that they came to a lot of the shows in his club and that this was the third time they'd been there to see me. That sounded very nice, so I took them up on their offer and joined them at their table.

The conversation was pleasant enough and after a while one of them mentioned fishing. I enjoyed fishing and back in those days I did a lot of it myself. When I told them that, they suggested that I come back to their house and see the prize fish that the homeowner had caught and had mounted over his fireplace. They said it was a short drive, about twenty minutes. It was about 1:00 a.m. They seemed like good people, and what else are you going to do in Cleveland at 1:00 a.m. when you're wide awake after a show? I agreed to go with them.

We piled into their car and I took a seat between a couple—I'll call them Mr. and Mrs. Bickerson. It probably should've been a red flag that I was sitting between the husband and the wife, but it was the middle of the night and we were going to look at a stuffed fish. Enough said. As things progressed, I got the feeling that all may not have been well in the Bickerson household. In fact, they subtly seemed to hate each other.

When they said it was a twenty-minute drive they were being optimistic, but we finally arrived at their house and, sure enough, there was a huge sailfish mounted and displayed over the fireplace. It doesn't take a long time to look at a stuffed fish, and there's really not a lot you can say about it, so we sat down and had a couple of drinks. Alcohol is an interesting substance. It's the liquid that can turn Dr. Jekyll into Mr. Hyde. I'm not a big drinker, but I drink socially and I don't criticize people for drinking or not drinking. However, over the years I have learned to be cautious about who I tip a glass with. This particular evening was part of the learning experience.

About 3:30 a.m., Mr. Bickerson called my name and motioned to me to join him near the staircase. He was standing on the landing with two kids at his side, ages about six and eight years old, wearing pajamas and wiping their tired eyes. He said to them, "You know who that is down there? That's Ed Sullivan!" I knew the kids were way too young to know who that was and, in fact, the sleepy kids looked like they wouldn't have cared if I were Santa Claus.

I said, "Ah, c'mon, let them go back to bed."

"You wanna walk back?!" he bellowed at me.

So I did Sullivan. "Here we go. It's gonna be a really big show!" And then I continued in Ed's voice, "And it's time for me to go back."

"Not until you've had breakfast," he said flatly, apparently not interested in whether or not I was actually hungry. Trapped.

During breakfast I was told that Mr. Bickerson was going to drive me back to the hotel, so I knew I only had to hang on a little longer. Eventually, we got into the car with Mr. Bickerson behind the wheel and me in the passenger seat. We were finally ready to go when I heard Mrs. Bickerson yell, "Wait, wait!" as she came running toward the car with her apron flying in the breeze. She motioned for me to roll down the window, which I did, then she grabbed my face and gave me a l-o-n-g, wet kiss on the mouth. Mr. Bickerson managed to roll up the window without decapitating her, although that might've been his intent. She jumped clear of the car and off we went. Mr. Bickerson drove me back to the hotel without saying one single word. The longest thirty-five minutes of my life.

One of the drawbacks of the show business life is that you end up working on a lot of holidays, particularly if you work the casino hotels or nightclubs. People who don't have to work on a holiday often want to be entertained. So *you* work. That's not a complaint, it just goes with the territory, but the fact of the matter is everyone likes to be with their family on the holidays, entertainers included. I don't care how nice the room that the casino gives you is, it always seems a little bland and lonely on a holiday.

I was working the Playboy Club in Great Gorge, New Jersey, one Thanksgiving. It was a nice resort and a good place to work, but don't let the whole Playboy thing fool you. We didn't spend our off-hours chasing bunnies around, and besides, even bunnies go home for Thanksgiving. I met some people after the show on Thanksgiving Eve and they invited me to come out to their home the next day for Thanksgiving dinner. They seemed like very nice people and the idea of spending a holiday with a family, even if it wasn't my own family, seemed a whole lot better than sitting in my hotel room having a turkey dinner from room service.

The day started out pretty well. My hosts were cordial, the dinner was tasty, and I was having a reasonably good time. Then the alcohol kicked in. The ladies had all put on aprons and headed for the kitchen to clean things up, leaving the men in the living room. One of the husbands had been knocking them back with great regularity, and he slumped into a chair with his drink and stared at me for a while. Finally he said slowly, "If you're so great, what are you doing here?"

I wish he would've asked me that question before I got in the car.

It didn't take too many experiences like this to make me cautious about joining fans for drinks and dinner. We tell our children not to take candy from strangers. I guess the same philosophy applies to traveling comics, on a slightly different level. At any rate, I decided that spending my off-hours alone was a better choice than spending them with people who might undergo a horrible personality change in the middle of the night. I began my program of self-protection by arranging for a taxi to take me both to and from the hotel, rather than waiting to get any bad news about who was going to drive me back after my show. I put the brakes on meal invitations as well, and I succeeded in my quest for private holiday meals on the road for quite some time. But I let down my guard once and ended up with a very interesting experience.

Several years later, while working a Playboy Resort in Lake Geneva, Wisconsin, eighty-two miles from Chicago, I was approached by one of the managers. He told me about a family that wanted me to join them for a 4th of July bash. He said they were having it at their beautiful lakeside home. He told me it was a beautiful setting, great barbecue, a band, games, etc., and they were going to send a helicopter to pick me up. A helicopter! That certainly beat going to see a stuffed fish, so I decided to take the risk.

At the precise time I was told to expect him, their pilot landed the copter softly on the Playboy Resort landing strip, and as we took off he proceeded to show me how he just followed the winding road below to the scene of the party.

What a sight it was! We landed on the designated place on the beautiful dark green, two-acre lawn. I felt as though I was in the midst of a wonderful dream—the colors, the happy people, kids and dogs running around, lawns decorated in American flags, streamers, music, the lake, and the aroma of picnic barbecue filling the air. Wow, what a day at the lake! The food was first-class and I even learned to really like something that I didn't think sounded any good. You want to be polite when you're a guest, so when they offered it to me and said, "Go ahead, try it!" . . . I did. It was peanut butter smeared over corn on the cob. Those were two foods I had never dreamed of combining, but it was surprisingly very tasty. Live and learn.

After thanking everyone for a wonderful afternoon, I happily boarded the copter and watched the beautiful scene fade away as we ascended and headed back to the resort. That afternoon broke the spell of never again wanting to join folks on their turf for food and drinks. There's not a 4th of July that I don't, at least for a second or two, reflect on that great afternoon.

Returning home, I couldn't wait to introduce my kids to that great taste of peanut butter with corn on the cob. They tried a few bites . . . and I got, "No, Dad, it's not for me." Four times. I guess whatever taste buds I have that it appealed to aren't hereditary. You can lead a horse to water . . . I suppose the moral of this story is, there are a few weird people in the world, but the good ones more than make up for them. And to never say never again, especially if it's going to be outdoors.

# Chapter Seventeen

## *Wacky Woody to Hecklesville*

Psychologists say that public speaking is one of the things people fear most. It's either first or second on the list along with death. That's some serious fear. With that in mind it seems to reason that people who perform in public are a little different from the rest of the folks. I think comics may be the most different of the different because we usually stand on stage alone, unlike actors in a play who are part of a cast. There's something that makes us want to do it, some experience good or bad that creates a need in us to stand in front of people and hold their attention. In my case, it's pretty easy to figure out. As one of six children, performing won the attention of my parents, which was my first goal, but it also helped out every time I changed schools, and when I was in the navy, and, eventually, when I needed to make a living. I'm pretty simple to figure out that way.

For other comics and performers the need may have come out of pain. The obese child who's picked on in school but becomes popular by being funny, for example. There's a lot of different reasons that may cause a person to become a performer, and it's not uncommon for the person you see on stage to be entirely different off stage. Take Johnny Carson. He was the absolute master of late-night television and most people would think he would be a blast to hang out with but, as I mentioned earlier, Johnny was shy. Pretty much the exact opposite of what you would expect. My point here is that there is something in performers that makes them view the world a little differently from everyone else. That can make for some unusual moments, both on stage and off.

Woody Allen is an interesting example. He's a very talented actor, comedy writer, and director. In his early career he got a lot of attention playing nerdy, nebbish characters that were incompetent and fragile. While this made him endearing on screen to a lot of people, his personal life ended up drawing a lot of negative attention that rubbed people the wrong way. There was a lot more going on with him than met the eye. I worked with him once and the experience was, well, unique.

Woody had gotten a special on the *Kraft Music Hall*, a series that usually did pretty high-quality shows. He was just starting to break through as a performer with that character that was always trapped in some kind of anxiety, but he was pretty well known as a comedy writer and he was also writing the show. I was invited to take part, along with Liza Minnelli, Mahalia Jackson, and William F. Buckley Jr. Liza and I performed in three separate sketches, which we rehearsed in a rehearsal hall in Manhattan, and the show was taped at a studio in Brooklyn. The rehearsal process was fairly typical: read first day, on its feet second day, etc. I believe we rehearsed for two weeks before the taping day, which took place with a live audience. I mention the live audience because the presence of an audience seemed to do something to Woody, and not in a good way. He became a bit nasty/sneaky, or you might call it physically overactive, with me suddenly becoming his punching bag.

The show was called "Woody Allen Looks at 1967," and we shot it near the end of that year. If you were around back then you remember that there was a whole lot of change going on in the country. Politics, music, and especially fashion. Clothing styles changed for the daring and miniskirts were in. Some loved them and some thought they were scandalous, but they were everywhere. In one sketch, Liza played Woody's wife and the two of them were going on a double date with me and my wife, played by April Nevens. Liza made her entrance in a miniskirt and told Woody she was ready to go. Woody, in his typical character, became a stuttering emotional wreck and told her to go back and put on a decent dress. The argument began.

At this point I made my entrance, arriving alone, before my wife, and made a gigantic fuss over the short skirt and her great legs. Woody reacted by moving me away from his wife while telling me how he felt about the outfit. During the numerous rehearsals Woody put his hands on my shoulders and moved me back a few steps. During the taping in front of the live audience, however, he more than moved me—he slammed me against a wall, knocking a few props off a shelf. Not satisfied when I rebounded off the wall from the first impact, he shoved me again. I was surprised, but I remained cool. No big deal, I figured, he's probably nervous, or thinks it's a funnier look if overdone. It would've been nice to have a little warning, but sometimes you really find comedy in the moment, so I let it go.

The middle sketch went smoothly; we had no reason to make contact in that one. It was the final sketch when I realized he had something against me that had to be dealt with privately. Unfortunately, we didn't do it privately. The sketch was a takeoff of a popular movie that came out that year, *Bonnie and Clyde*. Woody played Clyde, and of course Liza was Bonnie. The sketch was based on the part of the movie where they are holed up in a cabin, hiding from police. I played Clyde's brother, the part Gene Hackman played in the movie.

The physical part was where the brother drove a few others to the cabin to visit Bonnie and Clyde. As in the movie, when they saw each other for the first time in a while, rather than hugging, they did as many country guys do, a bit of open-hand light fisticuffs around the shoulders and arms to each other. So it was at rehearsal each time. A nice gentle little slap fight. When it came time to do the sketch in front of the audience, Woody changed it. We got to the greeting, and instead of a few slaps on the shoulders Woody gave me such a shot to the stomach. I immediately nailed one back to his midsection, buckling his knees. It was partially anger and partially reflexive. If someone punches you, you punch him back. Whoever was in charge of the show wisely decided not to reshoot the scene, so if you ever get a chance to see it, on YouTube or wherever things like that go, you can see Woody collapse and fall to one knee as the scene fades out. He's not acting. That's the real deal and it's all there for the world to see. I haven't seen or talked to him since. Would you?

Rod Steiger was a terrific actor with many memorable performances. As I mentioned in an earlier chapter, I used an impersonation of his distinctive voice and delivery in my first improv sketch. Steiger made an impact on me the first time I saw him on the screen. I was stationed in San Diego aboard the sub rescue vessel *Florikan*, which was tied up at the foot of Broadway. I was off duty one afternoon, so I wandered up Broadway to see a new movie, a western called *Jubal* that starred Glenn Ford as a character named Jubal Troop. There was an actor in the film who I had never seen or heard of before—Steiger—and I was fascinated by his acting and delivery. At a point in the film they thought Jubal was dead and Steiger announced it in a drawn-out vocal inflection that got my attention. I've never forgotten it: "Jubal Troop is deaaad!" I began to impersonate him to any of my shipmates who had ever heard of him. Over the years he became part of my act when his voice fit my purpose.

Years passed. I was at a cocktail party in Los Angeles where there were a number of actors, and one of them was the one and only Rod Steiger. I mentioned to a friend at the party that I had never met him, and the friend said he knew him and immediately took me over to introduce me. He was standing alone and he was a lot taller than I expected him to be. Anyway, my friend introduced us, we shook hands, and then my friend said something I wasn't expecting. "John does an impersonation of you." Steiger looked at me. "Do you do me from *The Pawnbroker*?" I answered that I didn't. "Then you don't do me." Oh, okay. That was that. Conversation over. For the record, Steiger was wonderful in *The Pawnbroker* and apparently considered it his greatest role. But when it came to me, if we weren't talking about *The Pawnbroker* we weren't talking.

Growing up on Long Island isn't like growing up in Hollywood. You're not likely to run into your favorite movie star at the hardware store. At one point during the Biener family road trip that was a recurring theme in my youth, we were able to move to the four-room apartment on the second floor of my sister Miriam and her husband Stan's two-story home on the corner of Morris Avenue and Dartmouth Street in Rockville Centre, Long Island, New York. I was about thirteen years old at the time, and I've always considered Rockville Centre my hometown. There was a bedroom that Tom and I shared, and one that Christine and Mom shared, along with a living room, bathroom, and an eat-in kitchen. Room enough for everyone, no problems.

One of the rumors floating around town was that comedian Alan King's home was in the wealthier part of our town. We, as kids, were on the lookout for him, since a good celebrity sighting could perk up an otherwise mundane afternoon. We kept our eyes peeled, but in the four years I lived there before joining the navy we never saw him once. After returning home from the service I'd see him on television, and I enjoyed his humor. He'd talk about airlines, and banks, and other areas of life that I hadn't heard made fun of by any other stand-up comic before as he clutched his ever-present cigar with one hand while the thumb of his other hand was tucked in his vest.

A few years go by, I've had a few different jobs, I've got a wife and three of my four kids, and I'm now a card-carrying comedian myself, hired at one point to entertain a convention crowd along with none other than Alan King. The affair was being held in one of the massive convention halls in the Hilton Hotel in Manhattan. I showed up wearing my rented tuxedo and reported to the gentleman who was to guide me to the correct ballroom. He took me to one side of a room that was divided by a partition. I could hear the muffled sound of the audience on the other side of the wall while I waited alone in the dimly lit, basketball court–sized room to be called to perform. I could hear introductions and the din from applause, chatter, and the like. Just me, the only table, long as it was, had two chairs. The rest of the huge space was empty.

I heard a door open at the far end of this enormous room and saw a guy walking toward me. As he got closer I realized it was Alan King, also in a tux, with a vest. I introduced myself, and gestured to the other chair. He refused, saying he didn't want to wrinkle his trousers, so he stood opposite me, telling me about his big house, garages, Rolls Royce, wine cellar, and other wonderful things about the place. He gave me a full rundown on what it was like to be a prosperous performer. Maybe he was bragging, maybe he was being encouraging, maybe just making conversation. I don't know. Then at one point, realizing I was to go on first, he excused himself to make a call and went looking for a pay phone. He walked all the way back to the door he entered from, then a few minutes later came walking back. When he got about twenty feet from me he asked, "Do you have a dime?" As he walked back with the change I gave him, I thought, *Wow, all that stuff and he couldn't come up with a dime.*

Some years went by when I was invited to appear on the new *Saturday Night Live with Howard Cosell.* Cosell was another interesting guy. He was primarily known as a sportscaster, starting out in the '50s with a career that extended into the '80s, but he also turned up frequently on non-sports shows. He had a big enough name and a strong personality, so he seemed like a pretty good choice to front the new show. It was an Ed Sullivan type of show, with the big difference that there were occasional comedy sketches. I had my material ready to do my stand-up act, but I was asked if could assist in a sketch that regular writer/comedian/actor Bill Murray was to do on the show. Sounded like fun, so I agreed.

A meeting was set up in the offices of the head writer for the show, which turned out to be none other than Alan King. I was told they wanted me to impersonate Mr. Cosell. Cosell had a unique delivery, the kind of thing an impressionist could really exaggerate for a laugh. The only problem was, I didn't

happen to impersonate Cosell and I wasn't sure I could get
him down on short notice. They told me that I should get as
close as I could, and that would be fine. After that was settled,
Alan went back to his desk, sat down, and asked us to tell
him, of all things, about the first girl we kissed when we were
young kids. We all took turns, and he seemed to get a big kick
out of our "confessions," and that was that.

The next day I had to "be" Cosell, so I had to come up with
something quickly. In a general way, Cosell's voice reminded
me a bit of John Wayne, so I did John Wayne's voice, slightly
sped up, without the mid-sentence pauses, and it got by just
fine with the audience. I believe the show lasted only a few
months and was gone just that quickly. That's showbiz.

I was originally asked to be on the premiere Howard Cosell
one-hour variety show, but a week before the taping date I got
a call from Howard asking me if I wouldn't mind giving up
my spot to Frank Sinatra. They wanted to open with Sinatra
instead of this kid? Sure, why not? Give the guy a break.
Sinatra drew a huge audience, of course, and they booked me
a week or two later. I had fun and everyone was happy. Who
could ask for more than that?

Hecklers are the curse of performers, particularly stand-
up comedians. We're on stage, usually alone, when someone,
usually drunk, will decide they want to try to be funnier than
we are. It's not just about the interruption, either. Comedy
is all about timing, and when someone throws your timing
off good material can sound not so good. Also, you want to be
thinking about your performance and not wondering if some
idiot is going to keep breaking into your act. It's an aggravation
for the audience, too. They came to hear the performer, not a
drunk. In most venues they have someone assigned to handle
hecklers. At the first or second interruption they'll politely

ask them not to do it again. If they continue they're likely going to be escorted out. That's helpful, but you still have to get the audience back where you want them.

In the mid-1970s, I opened for talented singer-dancer Ben Vereen at The Latin Casino, a very large night club in Cherry Hill, New Jersey. Members of the New Jersey roofer's union decided to have their annual party there and had bought out the opening evening of our two-week engagement. While waiting for my call to go on, my manager, Harry Colomby, stopped by the dressing room to tell me that it was going to probably be a rowdy crowd. He said I might have some trouble getting their attention, since a lot of the union members were sitting on tables with bulges in their tux jackets. He figured they weren't pouches of pipe tobacco. The audience was packing heat and all of them were trying to talk above the din. This was a tough looking and sounding bunch, to say the least.

"Five minutes, Mr. Byner!" said the stage manager as he knocked on my door. A couple of minutes later I stood behind the curtain and the noise from the crowd was loud. Really loud. I was introduced, the curtain opened, and I entered to absolutely no applause, just the din of a few hundred men loudly talking to each other. I stood there for what seemed to be a long time, when out of the noise, God sent some guy with an extremely loud voice from way in the back of the room to yell out, "What are you going to be when you grow up?" (Obviously directed at my five-foot-eight-inch height.) I yelled back, "Not a loud mouth!" This wasn't what the heavily armed, alcohol-fueled crowd was expecting. They immediately hushed and sat down in their seats to hear the show. Magic!

After my set, Harry came back to the dressing room to tell me that when I yelled back to the guy, the owner of the club, who had been standing with him in the back of the house, said to him "What, is John crazy?!" I sure was, but it paid off. And I didn't have to ask my dry cleaner to get powder burns out of my suit.

Another heckler experience that stands out didn't quite turn out that well. It happened in Great Gorge, a Playboy resort outside of Chicago. I was there with my then twelve-year-old son, Don. I used to take one child at a time on the road with me to spend some quality time with them. The kids got to travel a little bit, and everything was great.

On this trip Don picked out a model airplane at the airport gift shop to assemble at the resort, and we'd work on it after a show or on rainy days. The shows went great all week and life was good.

Saturday night came around and the club was packed. I was introduced and walked out onto the two-foot-high platform of a stage to see that the house trio was there and ready to go. The club management had really packed the audience in. In front of me there were long tables with at least five couples on each side, front to back. A guy sitting at a front table had his right foot propped up on the stage. I greeted the crowd and smiled at the guy, like "Yeah, I see you." I hoped that would be enough for him and began my intro to whatever I had planned for the show.

The guy said something to me, which I didn't pay any attention to, but as I continued, so did he. "Whatya gonna sing for?!" and "Don't do that!" kept popping out of his mouth until it was "All right already" from me. It wasn't just me who was bugged. People were shushing him and there were whispers of "Hey, shut up over there" and such. At this point the guy had gone from being a minor aggravation to a major distraction.

The trio and I kept looking for the bouncer or someone to show up while proceeding with the planned program. As I said before, I never was, or was thought to be, or wanted to be, Don Rickles. We were friends, I worked with him and enjoyed his humor, but you know what I mean? I'm not interested in putting people down. Oh, I have a few zingers up my sleeve, but I really don't like to get into that kind of thing. However, this guy was doing his own show to Lord knows who, 'cause those behind him looked as though they were on the wrong train . . . looking for the exits. I will also remind you that my act was always without anything that could embarrass someone, or insult anyone.

Now, with that in mind, after fifty minutes of his nonstop heckling, I finally stopped and said to the wannabe comic, "What do YOU want to talk about?"

"Sex," he shouted.

I, in disgust, said, "Well for you, that would be jerking off in your socks!" With that I "dropped the mic," walked off the stage, and went directly back to my suite. On entering, Don knew by the look on my face that something was different. So much for quality time with the family.

I felt drawn, just defeated and miserable. He said, "Come on, Dad, let's work on the model!" and we did, but I just couldn't shake the feeling I had. I thought of quitting the clubs, calling my agent, and all those dumb things one thinks of when the job, or someone, or something rubs you the wrong way. I don't know about your lives, but imagine you work hard to get something right and then someone comes in to ruin it for their own amusement. That's the way I felt.

As they used to say on the radio dramas, "The next morning . . ." I received a call from one of the King Sisters, the trio that was opening the show. She invited Don and me to join them for a picnic lunch alongside the golf course that day. I accepted her kind invitation and off Don and I went. We spread out the blanket, opened the nicely assembled baskets of food and drinks the Playboy club had put together for us, and enjoyed the day. No one mentioned the night before, and I wasn't sure if they had even heard about it.

While sitting with one of them on a blanket, not wanting to reflect on it, two guys with golf bag pull carts walked over to us, and after saying hello, one said to me, "We drove from Detroit to see you, John. Sorry about last night. If it makes you feel any better, we followed that guy into the men's room and gave him a stomachache!" They smiled, waved, and continued on with their game. They paid good money for their tickets. I guess they figured if they didn't get their money's worth in entertainment, they would at least get it in vengeance.

I don't normally condone that kind of thing, but I have to admit that in this case I felt relieved that justice was done. Before the show that evening the maître d', a blond, crewcut guy with a German accent, knocked on my dressing room door. He said he was sorry. He went on to say, "It was because the tables were so close together. I couldn't get to him to throw him out, and with all those people with him it would have been upsetting to the others." I grunted and he walked out. The next evening I learned he was fired. By the way, Don and I completed the model plane—a happy close to that encounter.

I was a heckler once. Sort of. Ed Sullivan had put together a show at Harrah's Club in Lake Tahoe, and I was on it along with comic Bob King. After we did our show one night we ran into British singer Matt Monro and the three of us decided to go across the street to the Sahara Lounge where Shecky Greene was performing. We were given a booth in the back and we settled in to watch his show. Shecky knew that Ed and all of us were in town, of course, but he didn't know Bob, Matt, and I were in his audience. Shecky got off a few zingers about Ed, and when that had gone on for a while I called out, in Ed's voice, *"Hi there, Shecky!"* He didn't see that one coming. He just stood there with his mouth hanging open while the audience had a huge laugh. Shecky and I later became friends and remain so today. We used to catch one another in the showrooms of Las Vegas, and today we continue to joke over the telephone.

Sometimes you have a packed house and the crowd goes wild, and occasionally things go the other way. I was working at the legendary jazz club Birdland in 1966, opening for John Coltrane and his trio. That should've been a great gig, but the fortunes of Birdland were going up and down, and I managed to hit it in one of the down cycles.

The focus of Birdland was music, of course, but I did impressions of many of the great jazz singers so I was usually a pretty good fit in clubs like this. I was also a big fan of John Coltrane, so I was ready for an enjoyable night. The MC at Birdland was a little person. He wore a tuxedo, announced the acts, and generally did his best to keep things moving in the right direction. I noticed he had an interesting habit. If he didn't like someone he'd mangle their name when he introduced them. Some sort of revenge, I guess.

Before I went on I could tell by looking at the room that I might be in for a tough night. When the MC announced me and I took to the stage it was confirmed. There weren't a lot of people in the room. Off to one side I could see into the bar—sort of. Actually, I could only see the legs of the people who were sitting at the bar, and the legs were all women and the women all appeared to be hookers. Sitting right in front center was a "jazz fan," drugged up and nodding out. There was nothing I could do but get on with it, so I performed to hooker legs and a junkie. I was on stage for about fifteen minutes without a laugh when I launched into my Tony Bennett impersonation. To my surprise, the jazz fan raised his head for a second and shouted, "Hey Tony!" He then nodded out again. After I got off stage Harry Colomby came up to discuss the second show. "Harry," I told him, "There's not going to be a second show."

I love working with singers and musicians for a couple of reasons. I enjoy music, so I make a pretty good audience when I'm not performing, but I also impersonate singers. When I'm working with a music act, I know they will have great musicians, which means I will get great accompaniment for my act.

General Motors had a big corporate event at the Hilton International Hotel in Las Vegas, and I was booked to work with Steve Lawrence and Eydie Gormé. This was a little unusual for corporate shows, since we performed for three nights. After the first night I ran into Steve Lawrence backstage after I finished my act and he said, "She [Eydie Gormé] really likes you." I thanked him for the compliment and then headed back to my room. The second night after my performance I ran into Steve again. This time he said, "Eydie said, 'Listen to this guy! He's great!'" Again a thank-you for the compliment and again I went back to my room. The same thing happened the third night, but this time Steve said, "If you weren't so shy we'd have you over." I knew I was a quiet guy, but I guess sometimes I may be a little too quiet.

# Chapter Eighteen

### *That's a Wrap?*

Fate, luck, whatever you want to call it, it shined on me. I was in the right place at the right time and a door into the world of show business opened just a crack. I walked through it without knowing where I was going, but I'm pleased with the journey's twists and turns.

One of the things I'm proud of is that I always managed to keep my life in balance and remember the things that are really important. Show business can be wonderful and exciting, but it can also be all-consuming. Long ago, when I was first starting out, a well-meaning friend suggested that I spend all my time with people who could help my career. To him, it was all about the gig and devoting time to the Hollywood social circle, which he said would help me become a success. True for some, I suppose, but that really depends on your personal definition of what success is. I love being in front of an audience and I love the laughs and applause, but that is part of my life, not all of it. I honor and appreciate those artists that dedicate their lives to the world they love, but I have had more than one friend who became a "success" by missing Real Life.

I don't want to sound like I'm antisocial, because that is not true at all. Yes, I'm a bit shy, and sometimes that gets in the way of social opportunities. Frankly, I give myself a B- in the smalltalk department. For example, I was at one of those big Hollywood events one night, waiting in the lobby for the doors to open. I was having a nice, relaxed conversation with Improv Comedy Club owner Budd Friedman, whom I've known for decades. Suddenly, out of the crowd, Lynn Redgrave walked over to us. Budd quickly introduced us and then rushed off to do something, leaving me to search my numb brain for something, anything, to say to that fine actress. I came up completely blank and we ended up staring at one another. Finally, after a few seconds that felt like years, she lowered her head and stepped past me with a "Mmm, bye-bye."

Although the Hollywood party scene can be a lot of fun, and I've certainly attended my share of great evenings with great people over the years, there are drawbacks on making that the center of your life. For me, a Hollywood party could include a deadly late-night drive up the fog-shrouded Pacific Coast Highway to my ranch, where I had to check on my animals, get a few hours sleep, and then wake up early to get the kids off to school. Sometimes it's just better to stay home. I can't think of one single Hollywood event that I regret missing, but I certainly would regret any time I missed spending with my kids for the sake of going to a party. I wanted a balanced life, but the balance was always tilted toward my family.

On my first movie I mistook a pause for an end. I won't do that twice. As they say, "It ain't over till the rather stout lady sings." At this point in my career I'm semi-retired and have two agents, one on each coast. It's fun to occasionally land a role in a television drama, or a comedy spot. Just a few months ago I took part in a remake of black-and-white noir 1940s film *D.O.A*, which originally stared actor Edmond O'Brien. I played the role of Majak, a dealer of dangerous goods. Prior to that I played the father of a supposed victim of the devil in *Lore*, a six-part Netflix series drama set circa 1895. "Black Stockings" is the episode.

I've bowed out of the stand-up comedy clubs because I don't care for the venues. Dressing rooms have been replaced with "the green room" where comics, their agents, boyfriends, girlfriends, managers, and an assortment of other non-performers wait before, during, and after the show. That makes it a little hard to concentrate on what you're about to do. The alternative is to sit at the bar, in the owner's office, or retreat to the refuge of your car between shows. It's okay for some, but I've been there, done that. I don't need to do it again.

But life continues to be fun and exciting. I'm generally open to do most anything that has decent dialogue and feels like a fun project. I'll be out with my pals on the golf course when word comes to me that someone would like to know if I'm interested in playing a "you-name-it" in a movie. If it sounds like fun I do it. If not, I play another nine. I'm happy either way. My career may not have always been well-planned, but it made me the guy I am today . . . and I like me.

Having been encouraged by many and disappointed by few, I've made my way through the show business maze, and I'm proud to say that I'm loved by many. I have made a lot of friends along the way, a few gigantic mistakes with my choices of people at times, but for the most part it has been, and continues to be, creative and challenging.

I'm proud to report that my singer, actor, dancer wife, Annie Gaybis, is my best friend and has interests of her own to keep her busy. (And she has a website, anniegaybis.com.) My grown children, Sandra, Rosine, Donald, and Patricia, all love me and are my constant friends. I'll always be here for my fans and friends. I thank you for your "fanship" and friendship.

Thanks for reading,
J

# About the Authors

John Byner's TV career break happened in New York City on Merv Griffin's "Talent Scouts Show" in 1964. After great exposure on both Gary Moore and Steve Allen's variety shows in 1966 and 1967, he clowned around on Ed Sullivan's showcase program over two dozen times and Johnny Carson late-night haunt over three dozen times. He has lent his vocal library of voices to hundreds of cartoons and animated films.

Douglas Wellman was a television producer-director in Hollywood for 35 years, as well as the assistant dean of the film school at the University of Southern California. He is the co-author, of *Surviving Hiroshima: A Young Woman's Story* with Anthony Drago, and *Boxes: The Secret Life of Howard Hughes* with Mark Musick. He currently lives in Southern Utah with his wife, Deborah.